USIN
EVALUATION
in Training and Development

Lea
This boc
anothe
upon

Plea
bc

⌈

19. 99

USING EVALUATION
in Training and Development

Leslie Rae

**KOGAN
PAGE**

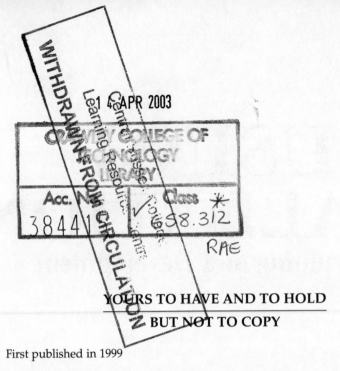

Kogan Page Limited
120 Pentonville Road
London N1 9JN, UK
and
Stylus Publishing Inc.
22883 Quicksilver Drive
Sterling, VA 20166, USA

British Library Cataloguing in Publication Data

A CIP record for this book is available from the British Library.

ISBN 0 7494 2805 8

Typeset by JS Typesetting, Wellingborough, Northants
Printed and bound in Great Britain by Biddles Ltd, Guildford and King's Lynn

Contents

Contents

or interview?; Telephone follow-up interviews; Critical
incident analysis; Learning logs; Repertory grid;
Longer-term evaluation; The competence stepladder;
Longer-term evaluation format

Preface

The purpose of this book is to provide comprehensive information and material about the validation and evaluation of training, produced in a format that it is hoped will be easy to use. The book should be useful for:

- training managers who need to know about validation and evaluation and who become involved in its processes;
- training managers who need material on which to base influencing presentations on evaluation to senior and line managers of their organizations;
- trainers who are very much immersed in the process of validation and evaluation and who need to practise it in addition to being required to make influencing presentations to their managers, line managers and sometimes senior managers;
- line managers who should be involved in the evaluation process with their staff who take up training and development opportunities, and who also may/should be involved in the design and implementation of evaluation together with the training department;
- senior managers who need to know what their training departments and line managers should be providing them with so that they can assess the worth and value of the organization's training programmes;
- consultants who are asked (not sufficiently frequently) by their client organizations to build effective evaluation into their contracts;
- people, usually trainers at different levels, who are seeking the Training and Development National Vocational Qualification (TD NVQ) at Levels, 3, 4 or 5 in which evaluation is a key area;
- all staff of an organization who need, within the requirements of Investors in People, to evaluate the training in their organization;
- anyone who is seeking an educational or vocational qualification that includes a requirement to understand and perhaps practise evaluation.

The evaluation of training and development programmes is probably one of the most discussed but least practised subjects in the training field. A survey by the Industrial Society in 1997 showed that, although 84 per cent of the organizations surveyed use 'happiness sheets – see Chapter 8) at the end of courses, a much lower proportion follow an effective evaluation process as described in this book. However, it is so important in the training cycle that the National Council for Vocational Qualifications, when it was researching the initial contents of the TD NVQ and found so little being practised, insisted that it became a significant part of the NVQ. Investors in People similarly insisted on its inclusion as an essential part of the process, and many educational and vocational qualifications linked to training and development include it as part of their learning processes.

Evaluation is not difficult, so why has it been practised so little? Probably the two principal reasons have been that:

1. It causes expense that can be ill afforded in a constrained financial era.
2. It takes time to practise, time that may be taken away from the practical function of training itself.

There is no disagreement with either of these criticisms, but they are not reasons for not performing evaluation. The most telling argument must be that without evaluation nobody really knows how effective any form of training might be. As a result, money may be spent unnecessarily. Consequently the time (within which the evaluation can be moulded to suit what is available) must be found, otherwise answers will not be possible to the questions that senior managers should be asking:

> How effective is your training? Can you prove it?
>
> Is your training worth what is being spent on it?
>
> Can you prove it?

This book sets out in a very practical way to try to help all those with these responsibilities and questions, either to ask or to answer. It follows the logical process of evaluation within the training cycle, following any training needs analysis, and starting in parallel with the design of the training itself.

Within this training cycle a comprehensive, practical and logically sequenced evaluation model is presented, intended to clarify and extend many of the existing models which, in many cases, leave something to be desired.

Evaluative measures, before the start of the training; at the start of the training; during the training; at the end of the training; and in the medium and longer term following the training, are all discussed. Guidelines are suggested, methods described and practical resources offered. The responsibilities of everybody who should be connected with the process are discussed, with particular reference to the greater parts that should be played by senior and line managers. Within the progressive process sections, subjects such as knowledge, skill and attitude tests; practical demonstration tests; activity and behavioural observation; techniques for determining how the event is progressing during the training programme; reactionnaires, questionnaires and action planning, are all discussed, with practical guidelines about how to do them. The on-the-job implementation of training and its link with medium- and long-term evaluation are emphasized, and the extremely difficult subject of the value effectiveness of training is approached. Concentration is on all aspects of learning, from self-instruction and direct training courses to programmed, distance, open learning.

Methods are not given as cast in stone, and alternative approaches are given wherever possible. Chapter 14 is concerned with customizing evaluation to suit your organization and the resources you can afford for the process – this is on the traditional basis that 'you cut your cloth according to your means', but 'you can only expect to get what you pay for'!

All the methods and resources are practical and practicable and have been used on innumerable training and development programmes in a variety of areas, the most recent in the introduction of an Inland Revenue new Trainer Development Programme that included a module on evaluation, and was also evaluated itself in the ways suggested. The module was based to a large extent on the material in this book.

Format

The book is structured in a reasonably logical and progressive format, starting with the reasoning behind the use of evaluation in training and development, then describing, in the logically progressive approach of the evaluation model, the practical steps that can be taken to achieve an effective evaluation process. The intention has been to make the content as practical and as usable as possible and checklists, summaries and example instruments should help in this process. The instruments are recommended suggestions but most can easily be modified to suit individual circumstances.

Acknowledgements

I should like to give my thanks to Philip Mudd and Will Mackie of Kogan Page Ltd for their continued valuable support and advice, and to Jacqueline Twyman of First Impressions for her assistance in ensuring that many deficiencies in the manuscript were avoided (I must still accept responsibility for the end result!).

Leslie Rae

I

What is Evaluation?

THE MACRO AND MICRO LEVELS OF EVALUATION

Evaluation, assessment, measurement, quality checking – or whatever term is relevant in the situation – are at the core of any effective organization. They answer the essential questions:

- Are we achieving the objectives set?
- Is the quality being achieved in accord with the standards set?
- Are the achievements being made in the most efficient and effective manner, and at the most economic cost?
- Are the individuals and the organization growing as a result of the essential continuous development of both?

MACRO LEVEL EVALUATION

The assessment of results at what might be considered the macro level is the relatively simpler process. For example, in a production environment, is the intended product being produced:

- within the required time and at the required time?
- to the agreed standards?
- at the most economic and agreed cost?

These criteria can be tested by checks on whether:

- the product is within the quality and quantity controls set up;
- the product satisfies the requirements of the customer in a positive manner – with some form of specific comment rather than the absence of complaint, which is no evaluation;
- the customer repeats the order as necessary.

In a similar way, the provisions of a service can be assessed at the final macro level by posing the same types of questions, albeit in rather more subjective terms.

MICRO LEVEL EVALUATION

Below this final product, macro level, the finer details of evaluation become more difficult, although they are essential in ensuring that the macro product is achieved. For example, it may be necessary, because of failings at the macro level, to show that a specific skill that is part of the macro process is being carried out:

- in the most efficient and effective way;
- at the lowest cost;
- with a high implementation value;

and that these aspects are being achieved by the training and development measures taken. It will also be necessary to demonstrate that the skill changes and improvements have occurred *because* of these measures rather than *without* (or perhaps in spite of) the training and development.

Evaluation at this micro level requires often complex, certainly extensive, and as objective as possible approaches and measuring instruments. In many cases where skills are involved, particularly at the higher levels of achievement, complete objectivity is not possible. For example, improvement changes in interpersonal skills cannot be subjected to the same rigorous, quantitative and objective measurements that were possible in the production of an object. Instead, more subjective approaches need to be used, accepting the subjectivity as the only *realistic* approach possible in the circumstances. This degree of subjectivity is often used as an excuse for not even attempting evaluation, but this is unacceptable. An attempt at evaluation, however, subjective, must be made, otherwise there is no 'evidence' whatsoever that what has been done has been effective in any way. After all, if the subjective measures are applied to similar situations in a consistent manner, a greater degree of 'objectivity' results.

THE CRITERIA FOR EVALUATION

In evaluation information on four criteria is essential as a minimum requirement:

1. **THE LEVEL OF THE LEARNERS PRIOR TO TRAINING**
2. **THE LEVEL OF THE LEARNERS POST TRAINING**
3. **CONFIRMATION OF THE EFFECTIVE IMPLEMEN-TATION OF THE LEARNING**
4. **EVIDENCE THAT THE IMPLEMENTATION CHANGES WERE AS A RESULT OF THE TRAINING**

1. The starting position of the learners must be known as a result of measurement or assessment, to the maximum extent possible. The comments above on objectivity and subjectivity must be applied in this case, the maximum extent possible depending on the nature of the event being assessed.
2. Following a period of learning, in whatever form, the completion position of the learners must be known in the same form and to the same extent as the position before the learning event started. Criteria 1 and 2 are the absolutely essential elements of evaluation of any nature: if the position before any action to effect an improvement is not known, it is impossible to assess what movement has taken place.
3. The learners put the learning into practice on their return to their workplaces, and this implementation is not only effective but results in a measure of change and/or improvement, for both the individuals and the organization, or part of it.
4. The effective learning change was in fact due to the training and development initiatives and would not have happened without them. Improvements can take place in the workplace without any apparent intervention, and can frequently be traced to a change in motivation and commitment rather than learning – perhaps as a result of rumours of redundancy or other forms of change. Or individuals themselves, without reference to the organization, decided to improve their knowledge and skills, separately from, and perhaps superior to, the developmental measures offered. It is essential if a claim for improvement is made based on the intervention of training and development that this change has in fact been due to this process, otherwise considerable costs can be incurred on false premises.

WHAT IS EVALUATION?

So far, the terms evaluation, assessment and measurement have been used, and in many ways the actual words do not matter. However, if a process is to be described and used in, say, an organization, everybody in that organization will benefit from a common language and terminology. In this book, I use 'evaluation' as the all-embracing term that includes the other expressions. This is not necessarily pedantically correct or fully descriptive, but it at least includes the other descriptions without having to apply arbitrary definitions to them.

The other common title used is 'validation' and, although this can be very expressive as a descriptive title, the user and listeners must be fully in accord about what is meant by this rather more restrictive definition. Some practitioners use 'evaluation' to describe the complete process, with any sub-elements being merely part of 'evaluation'. Others use 'validation' and 'evaluation', the former being seen as a sub-division, a part of the wider 'evaluation'. Some use 'validation' alone in place of 'evaluation', and so on.

If a more prescriptive definition is required, the following are widely accepted forms.

Validation

This can be seen as the assessment or investigation of the training and development process used to achieve learning and change. The training/learning process itself is 'validated' to ensure that the specific objectives of both the training programme and those of the learner are met. The questions asked will include:

- What terminal objectives were applied to the programme?
- With what terminal objectives did the learner commence the programme?
- Were the objectives of both the training programme and the learner met?
- Were the training methods used the most effective and appropriate?

It will be seen that the validation applies directly to the programme and its immediate results, with many sub-divisions within the general questions – were the objectives the appropriate ones?; were the learners who attended or completed the programme the appropriate ones?; could the learning have been achieved by the use of different training methods?; and so on. In other words the emphasis is on the immediacy of the training and learning, ensuring that the learners complete the training programme having achieved an effective change and improvement.

Evaluation

This takes in the wider aspect and, although including the validation of the learning event, looks particularly at issues concerned with the application of the learning in the workplace, its longer-term implementation and the cost and value effectiveness of the training and development provided.

Assessment

This term is frequently used instead of 'validation', but more often refers to the actual measurement of the extent of learning within a validated process. For example, an end of programme instrument that analyses the extent of the learning by seeking the learning levels of a number of subjects, in validating the training is also assessing the level of achievement.

WHY EVALUATE?

There can be little doubt that the implementation of an evaluation process in an organization involves the expenditure of time, money and resources, possibly very substantial expenditure if the evaluation is to be fully effective. Consequently the question 'why should we evaluate?' is often raised, rather than the more obvious initial question '*how* should we evaluate?'

Figure 1.1 summarizes the principal reasons given by any organization as to why it should not go ahead with an evaluation programme.

You have all heard (or made) some of these comments. The list is not exhaustive of the reasons (excuses?) put forward. Let's look at some of these excuses and lay their ghosts.

■ *It's not really possible to measure the results of a training programme. You either believe that it's successful or you don't.*

As suggested earlier, it is possible to evaluate *any* training programme, perhaps sometimes subjectively, but at least an attempt is being made. If you approach evaluation with the attitude of 'it can't be done', it won't be done. Internal beliefs are very fickle feelings which can be tempered by a range of events – at the end of a training course when everybody got on with each other, including yourself, it is easy to tell yourself that it was very successful, even if it hadn't been in objective terms.

- It's not really possible to measure the results of a training programme. You either believe that it's successful or you don't.
- Trainers know without all these forms whether their training course has been successful or not.
- Evaluation only really refers to training such as computer training where there is a definite, measurable end product.
- Evaluation is the responsibility of:
  - the training department (says line management);
  - line managers (says the trainer);
  - the training department and line management (says Personnel); and so on.
- Nobody has asked me to evaluate the programme, so obviously they're not interested.
- Evaluation wasn't raised by the client when the training arrangements were agreed (says the consultant).
- Evaluating all the training I do would take up so much of my time that I wouldn't be able to do the training.
- What more evaluation do you want? I hand out the questionnaire at the end of the course – isn't that enough?

Figure 1.1 *Principal reasons given for not evaluating*

- *Evaluation only really refers to training (such as computer training) where there is a definite, measurable end product.*

Agreed that this is so, but only to a certain extent. Computer program training; new procedure introduction training; machine operation training; and so on, all these can be evaluated with virtually 100% objectivity. But because other forms of training are not so susceptible to this ultimate evaluation, as we have seen earlier, this does not mean that evaluation is impossible, only rather more limited.

- *Evaluation is the responsibility of the training department (says line management); evaluation is the responsibility of line managers (says the trainer); evaluation is the responsibility of the training department and line management (says Personnel); and so on.*

This argument is usually used when the ones who are being asked to do the evaluation either feel they haven't time; are not interested in evaluation; or are frightened of what they might have to do and/or what the results may disclose! We shall return later to this subject: suffice to say at the moment that evaluation must be a shared process with a number of disciplines and levels making their relevant inputs.

■ *What more evaluation do you want? I hand out the questionnaire at the end of the course – isn't that enough?*

This is the syndrome of the trainer who hands out a 'happiness' sheet, two or three minutes before the end of the course, and expects the learners to complete it fully in that short time when their minds are probably only on returning home. This is not evaluation and it certainly isn't enough! The question to ask of any evaluation process is 'does it prove anything (proof being used in either the objective or subjective way as suggested)?' If it doesn't, the reasons are usually that it is insufficient and other steps should have been taken.

■ *Nobody has asked me to evaluate the programme, so obviously they're not interested (says the internal trainer)*
■ *Evaluation wasn't raised by the client when the training arrangements were agreed (says the consultant).*

These comments are linked, the emphasis depending on whether the training is being performed by the organization trainer or an external consultant. It may indeed be that the stakeholder or client has not suggested evaluation, but the wise trainer still does some form of evaluation – the maximum amount possible – as it is not unknown for the stakeholder or client to ask for evaluation at a later stage when it is no longer viable to do so. In any case, shouldn't the trainer be interested in knowing how successful their work has been? The external consultant is obviously at a disadvantage in these cases as they will usually have neither the time nor opportunity to follow the full processes of evaluation with the group involved. However, it is always worth raising the question of evaluation to obtain the client's views, and evaluation is so important that it should be brought to the client's attention. It is then up to them to decide whether it should be included or not.

■ *Evaluating all the training I do would take up so much of my time that I wouldn't be able to do the training.*

There is some legitimacy in this reason as evaluation does take up a substantial amount of time and resource if it is to be performed effectively. It is easy to respond 'can you afford not to do so?', but this is an incomplete response. If the trainer's time is taken up completely with providing training, the only alternatives are to:

- not perform any evaluation and use the time argument as the reason for so not doing
- convince the boss of the value of evaluation and negotiate time and resource to do it
- perform whatever evaluation can be squeezed in on the basis that some evaluation is better than none at all.

I believe that there are only two alternatives in most cases; either negotiate time to evaluate in an effective manner, or do nothing at all. The third option quoted above tends to develop into the 'happiness' sheet action, encouraging the belief that this is evaluation. But, as has been mentioned earlier, at the very least if you don't know where the learners have come from, how do you know that their journey has been worthwhile or successful?

Effective evaluation does take time, but with wider division of the responsibility for parts of it, the resource impact can not only be lessened but also improved. Perhaps the principal problem is building in time on the programme to include effective evaluation measures, but, as we shall see, there are ways to solve this 'problem'.

If training and development are to be effective, there *must* be some method by which they can be evaluated in an effective manner, otherwise we shall never know whether all the time, money and energy has really produced positive results. We can *feel*, *suspect*, or *guess* that the training and learning have been successful, but without an evaluative approach we shall never *know*.

REASONS FOR EVALUATION

When evaluation, or what is claimed as evaluation, does take place in an organization, a number of reasons are given about why it is done – some acceptable, others far from this.

The reasons listed in Figure 1.2 are all ones I have encountered in my training and development activities and in many cases – particularly the first two – the trainers concerned believed these were justifiable. Obviously they had been influenced by statements about the value of evaluation, but had accepted these for the wrong reasons. In the third and fourth reasons quoted, the trainers involved had little choice – this was of value provided that the evaluation they *had* to do or were continuing as the norm was effective. In some cases it

1. It's a 'good' thing to do
2. It looks good
3. Been told to do it
4. Always been done here
5. Part of TD NVQ requirement
6. Part of MEd (T & D) or similar requirement
7. Part of 'Investors in People' requirements
8. To improve effectiveness of training and development

Figure 1.2 *Reasons for evaluating*

was, but in other cases it amounted to little more than a 'happiness' sheet.

Reasons five, six and seven though, if only because of the requirements, at least ensured that the trainers/learners performed sufficient research and practice to ensure that they understood the real principles and reasons for evaluation, and hopefully this resulted in the installation and effective operation of the techniques.

Reason eight, even if taken on the face of the statement alone, must be the most acceptable reason. It implies understanding and acceptance of the underlying principles and the value of an evaluation practice, and includes at the least the minimum aspects of such a practice.

THE BENEFITS OF EVALUATING AND THE CONSEQUENCES OF NOT EVALUATING

The processes of either doing or not doing something, of whatever nature, all have consequences. We have seen the advantages of evaluating (and this theme will be returned to throughout this book). However, there are specific consequences of *not* evaluating that can be identified at this stage. If you consider that these are irrelevant, are not worth considering in your situation, or are unlikely to change your mind, feel free to ignore them. But if you are a trainer or a training manager, I suggest that you do so at your peril!

Figure 1.3 summarizes the benefits of evaluating and Figure 1.4 the consequences of not evaluating.

Most of the statements are self-explanatory; the following I feel require one or two comments.

- Training objectives met
- Client's objectives/needs met
- Learners' objectives/needs met
- Performance changed or improved
- Change due to effectiveness of training
- Learning transferred to work
- Required proof for sponsors

Figure 1.3 *Benefits of evaluation*

- Trainer self-assessment impossible
- Trainer assessment not possible
- Training design non-assessable
- Learners' reactions/learning unknown
- Learners blind to own change
- Change attribution not possible
- Learning transfer not assessable
- Senior sponsors not aware of success
- Valid responses not possible

Figure 1.4 *Consequences of not evaluating*

Consequences

'Learners blind to own change'

Particularly in training events that contain a lot of new or remedial material, learners who have limited reflecting skills may not realize what they have learned, or to what extent. If they are required to reflect on their possible learning, for evaluation purposes, this will help them to consolidate in their own minds what they have in fact learned.

'Change attribution not possible'

This refers to any uncertainty as to whether the change in operational practices by the learners has occurred as a result of the training or would have happened without any intervention.

'Senior sponsors not aware' and 'Valid responses not possible'

Whether or not the senior sponsors of the training have asked for evaluative measures to be taken, if an effective evaluation programme has been followed the analysis report can be sent to them to ensure that they know what is being achieved. Or if pertinent questions are posed voluntarily by the senior sponsors the trainer or training manager is in a position to respond immediately with valid data.

IS IT WORTH IT?

To answer a final query about evaluation to the trainer, the training manager and the organization, Figure 1.5 might be used to give an indication of the value of evaluating a particular training and development programme.

DOES IT NEED EVALUATING? IS IT WORTH IT?

Please read the following questions in relation to a particular course/programme/system you are currently or may be considering evaluating. In each case tick the alternative answer which is nearest in applicability.

1. **IN GENERAL, HOW IMPORTANT IS THE EXISTENCE OF THE TRAINING TO THOSE WHO ARE SPONSORING/ FUNDING IT?**

    4   Absolutely essential to their well-being
    3   A major priority of influential people at present
    2   Being given a certain amount of support and encouragement by influential people
    1   Very difficult to gauge how much support it really enjoys
    0   Rather surprising that it is still happening.

2. **THE PROGRAMME/COURSE/ACTIVITY IS DESIGNED SPECIFICALLY TO MEET THE NEEDS OF:**

    4   A wide range of people, most of whom are able to arrange their own funding

Figure 1.5   *'Is it worth it?' questionnaire*
(Adapted from Scriven (1974), and Easterby-Smith (1994)

3 A wide range of people funded by grants/awards/ subsidies/ budgets which look sound for the time being

2 A limited population, but for whom funding is relatively stable

1 A limited population with single source funding

0 No particular group and funding looks most uncertain.

3. HOW MUCH IS KNOWN OF WHAT VARIOUS 'STAKEHOLDERS' THINK OF THE PROGRAMME?

4 There is very reliable information on the views of major sponsors/funding bodies, etc about it

3 There is reasonable information about the opinions of primary stakeholders

2 It is possible to make informed guesses about opinions of some stakeholders and/or a little firsthand information from participants exists

1 There is very little information about what even participants think about it

0 It would be unwise to encourage anyone to think too much about their views of the programme.

4. HOW MUCH INFORMATION/EVIDENCE IS THERE ABOUT THE EFFECTS OF THE PROGRAMME?

4 Extensive information gathered from a number of sources over a long period of time

3 Adequate information has been gathered from 'reliable' informants

2 End of course questionnaires are sometimes used, and action plans/projects occasionally yield some information

1 People (and bosses) let us know when they are dissatisfied

0 No one has much of a clue.

5. HOW WELL IS THE RELATIONSHIP BETWEEN WHAT GOES ON IN THE PROGRAMME AND THE APPARENT EFFECTS UNDERSTOOD?

4 There is extensive knowledge about which parts of the programme have an effect, which don't and why

3 Participants have indicated which processes have led to

Figure 1.5 *'Is it worth it?' questionnaire (continued)*
(Adapted from Scriven (1974), and Easterby-Smith (1994)

which outcomes for them

2 There is some 'feel' for which aspects of the programme are more or less useful

1 It's very difficult to tell what causes what

0 We don't really know what actually happens in the relation-ship between the programme and application.

6. TO WHAT EXTENT HAS THE PROGRAMME BEEN EXAMINED IN RELATION TO ALTERNATIVE WAYS OF SATISFYING THIS APPARENT NEED?

4 There is clear evidence available that it is preferable to existing alternatives

3 There is some evidence that it better than most immediate competition

2 We know roughly what the similarities and differences are between this and alternative approaches

1 It is not clear how this compares with various alternative approaches

0 We have not really considered the possibility that there are other ways of doing this.

7. WHAT DO YOU REALLY THINK THOSE PEOPLE WHO HAVE HAD SOME CONTACT WITH THE PROGRAMME (PARTICIPANTS, BOSSES, SPONSORS) THINK ABOUT ITS VALUE?

4 It is of great value to the organization or individuals in general

3 It is of much value when combined with the right people in the right context

2 It can be quite useful on some occasions, but there are plenty of other ways of achieving just as much

1 Many people have reservations about its value

0 Most people are convinced it has no value.

Figure 1.5 *'Is it worth it?' questionnaire (continued)* (Adapted from Scriven (1974), and Easterby-Smith (1994)

A ROUGH GUIDE TO THE INTERPRETATION OF THE RESULTS, WHICH MUST BE LOOKED ON AS INDICATORS ONLY:

NUMBER OF '4s' ....   **NUMBER OF '3s'** ....

NUMBER OF '2s' ....   **NUMBER OF '1s'** ....

NUMBER OF '0s' ....

a   If most of your ringed answers are 4s or 3s this suggests that your organization, and particularly your senior management, are interested in the training function. Consequently they are likely to ask questions to which you must have clear and valid answers. In this case, evaluation or its active continuation is an essential part of your training activities.

b   If your answers are a mixture of 3s and 2s, this suggests that there is some doubt about the value of what you are doing and how you are doing it. You should consider conducting in-depth evaluation to answer the questions that particularly have a '2' response. Otherwise you could have difficulty in answering questions about whether you are approaching training in the most appropriate way.

c   If you have ringed answers to any of the questions at '2' or less, your courses, etc may be vulnerable, not just to questions, but to attack. You should consider conducting some evaluation in that area aimed at proving that the system works and is of value.

d   If you have answered '0' to many of the questions, then it is probably not worth bothering with evaluation because the system deserves to be wound up anyway.

Figure 1.5 *'Is it worth it?' questionnaire*
(Adapted from Scriven (1974), and Easterby-Smith (1994)

2

—

Evaluation in Training and Development and the Organization

Evaluation is not a singular exercise but an integral part of the training and development process and, as suggested in the previous chapter, should be the responsibility of a number of role holders in an organization. This chapter describes the place of the evaluation process in the training cycle, showing the ideal set of elements for an effective evaluation process, and also proposes the practical application of the 'training quintet' in an organization and the evaluation responsibilities of its members.

THE TRAINING CYCLE

The training cycle, whether we are considering direct training and development courses or other types of programme (such as open learning involving text, video, interactive video, or computer-based approaches), follows a similar process, the methods alone varying from one area to another. Figure 2.1 summarizes the units of this cycle, which starts with an identification or suspicion of a training or development need, and is completed with the final act of evaluation, the long-term confirmation that the learning achieved has been implemented successfully and is being maintained. In the figure evaluation processes are shown in black boxes and training processes in white boxes. Joint task and learning processes are shown in grey.

A PRACTICAL EVALUATION MODEL

As shown in Figure 2.1, a number of the activities are either evaluation activities or related to both the training and the evaluation. These (with

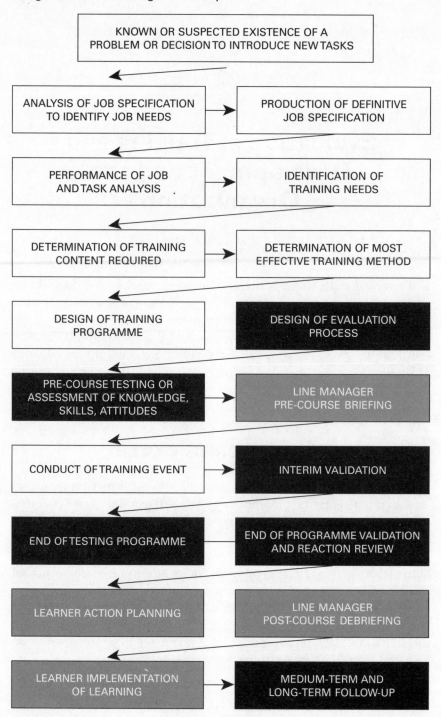

Figure 2.1 *The training cycle*

two additional items) number 14, and describe the evaluation model (see Figure 2.2).

Most models of evaluation processes describe only four or so items, usually applied to levels of evaluation. My model not only considers these levels, but also describes the logical and practical steps necessary to achieve an effective evaluation; hence the 14 steps.

1. Training needs analysis leading to training objectives
2. Design of the evaluation process
3. Pre-course testing or assessment of knowledge, skills and attitudes
4. Line manager pre-course briefing
5. Interim assessment and validation
6. End of programme testing
7. End of programme reaction review
8. End of programme validation
9. Learner action planning
10. Line manager post-course debriefing
11. Medium-term follow up
12. Long-term follow up
13. Cost and value effectiveness analysis
14. Assessment and report on achievement of the objectives

Figure 2.2 *The evaluation model*

The format of this book follows the logical process of this model.

The joint task and learning processes include the pre- and post-course briefing sessions between the line manager and the learner, and contributing to the evaluation process should be happening whether or not there are further evaluation measures being introduced.

It will be noted that the evaluation process is initiated early in the training cycle, almost at the very beginning if training needs analysis is seen as part of the evaluation process itself. Design of what, how and when the evaluation process should be integrated with the training must take place at the same time that the training itself is being designed – this emphasizes the integrated nature of the training and the evaluation.

The ideal situation is for any early testing or other assessment of the learners' existing knowledge, skills and attitudes to take place before the training itself starts. This reduces the time necessary on the programme for evaluation processes and also gives the trainers pre-knowledge of the existing levels of the potential learners – consequently the learning programme can be modified in the light of this inform-ation. There are obvious problems in ensuring that this pre-programme assessment takes place, not least of which relates to who should do it! The trainers may not have the time for what might involve extensive travelling to conduct the assessments; the line managers may not have the time, commitment or skill to do it themselves; and, if it is to be carried out by post, there has to be a foolproof method of ensuring completion and return sufficiently in advance of the training pro-gramme for the information to be of any use – not always an easy task. In practice, if it is done at all, it usually has to be done at the start of the learning programme itself.

OTHER EVALUATION MODELS

As indicated above, a number of evaluation models exist, the majority concentrating on what are described as the levels of evaluation (which are contained as an integral part in my model). Probably the best known, and certainly the most practicable, is the four levels model of Kirkpatrick (1996). Kirkpatrick embraces his four level model within a ten-step process for planning and implementing a training pro-gramme (cf my 19 stage training cycle).

The four levels are defined as:

```
Level 1 – Reaction
Level 2 – Learning
Level 3 – Behaviour
Level 4 – Results
```

Level 1 – Reaction

Evaluation at this level measures the *reaction* of the participants in the programme. This is quite different from the more scientific and objective assessment of the programme in *evaluation* respects, as there are so many subjective value judgements that can interfere with objectivity. In many ways, reaction assessment indicates the amount of customer satisfaction. Many evaluators decry reaction assessments because of this subjectivity, but to enable training and development programmes to continue to run and develop, the customers must be satisfied; otherwise the learning on the programme will suffer, and the demand for a programme that does not provide customer satisfaction, *in addition to effective learning opportunities*, will soon reduce significantly.

Level 1 is included in my model in stages 5 and 7.

Level 2 – Learning

Kirkpatrick defines learning in his model as the extent to which participants change attitudes, improve knowledge and/or increase skill as a result of attending the programme. He suggests that this learning can be evaluated by:

■ the use of control groups;
■ pre- and post-testing.

Level 2 is included in my model at stages 3 and 6, and to some extent at stage 8.

Level 3 – Behaviour

The evaluation of behaviour in this model is concerned with the extent of the transfer of knowledge, skills and attitudes following the learners' attendance on the programme.

Kirkpatrick advocates for this evaluation:

■ the continued use of control groups;
■ allowing time for the behaviour change to take place;
■ evaluating before and after the programme;
■ survey and/or interview the learners, their immediate superiors, their subordinates and any others who have the opportunity to observe their behaviour;
■ repetition of the evaluation at appropriate times;
■ consideration of costs versus benefits of this form of evaluation.

The activities suggested for this level are contained principally in my stages 9 to 12.

Level 4 – Results

Development of evaluation in this level extends the changes observed in Level 3 and includes an attempt to rationalize the value of the learning and its implementation at the place of work, in terms of the return on investment by the organization.

This is without doubt the most difficult of any level or stage of evaluation to attain results in an objective and quantitative manner. Level 4 is contained in my stages 9 to 14.

Kirkpatrick's model with its four levels gives an appearance of simplicity and ease of operation, but the few levels cloud the wealth of activity and difficulty within each one. When the constituents are broken down into their individual elements it will be seen that the model actually includes quite a number of the stages described in my model and this book.

THE NATIONAL VOCATIONAL QUALIFICATION

Trainers who want to be able to perform effective evaluation, but who are concerned at the time and resources that will be necessary, and the extent of evaluation required, can glean some guidance from the published standards for the UK's National Vocational Qualifications (NVQ). NVQ Standards have now been developed for a large number of occupation groups, so let us use the Training and Development NVQ (TD NVQ) as an example. The emphasis of the qualification is on practical activities carried out as part of the trainer's role, thus developing an effective trainer, rather than on academic qualifications.

The Standards described in the TD NVQ literature show that the qualification is divided into *Units of Competence*, each Unit relating to an area of the trainer's role. So we find that Key Role E2 (Evaluate the effectiveness of training and development programmes) contains three Units:

1. Unit E21   Evaluate training and development programmes.
2. Unit E22   Improve training and development programmes.
3. Unit E23   Evaluate training and development sessions.

These Units of Competence therefore require an NVQ candidate to have a wide, practical knowledge and skill in evaluation practices, the details of which are shown in the sub-divisions of the Units, the *Elements of Competence*. As an example, Unit E21 contains the Elements:

- ■ Element E211 Select methods for evaluating training and development programmes.
- ■ Element E212 Collect information to evaluate training and development programmes.
- ■ Element E213 Analyse information to improve training and development programmes.

Performance Criteria define how these functions can be seen to be carried out satisfactorily. For example, Element E211 has nine Performance Criteria:

Unit E21   Evaluate training and development programmes
Element E211 Select methods for evaluating training and development programmes

Performance criteria

(a) The training and development programmes being evaluated are clearly identified and used as the focus for the evaluation process.
(b) The specific objectives and desired outcomes of the training and development programmes are clearly identified.
(c) The purpose, scope and level of evaluation are clearly identified.
(d) Methods that are capable of evaluating training and development programmes are clearly identified.
(e) The advantages and disadvantages of each evaluation method are suitably assessed and an appropriate method selected.
(f) Evaluation criteria are appropriate to the training and development programme and clearly specified.
(g) Evaluation methods are capable of being implemented within the resources available.
(h) All aspects of the evaluation method are clearly identified and agreed with the appropriate people.
(i) A plan for implementing the evaluation is clearly specified.

In addition to the Performance Criteria listed, notes are included in the Element giving guidance on the type of evidence - performance and knowledge - required to satisfy the criteria. For the Performance Criteria described above the evidence required is:

Performance evidence

- identification of training and development programmes being evaluated;
- specification of evaluation methods and rationale for their selection;
- specification of evaluation criteria and rationale for their selection;
- explanation of scope and purpose of evaluation;
- plan for the implementation of the evaluation;
- notes of agreement made.

Knowledge evidence

- methods of evaluating training and development programmes;
- range of evaluation criteria available;
- how to identify criteria for evaluation;
- employment and equal opportunities legislation and good practice;
- relevant national and organizational debates concerning learning;
- relevant national and organizational debates relating to evaluation and quality improvement.

From the above it will be obvious that the Standards suggest substantial and in-depth knowledge and skill in evaluation are necessary for the effective trainer, and even if an individual is not going forward for the TD NVQ, the Standards outline the general competences required of a trainer. The principal application of the Standards is in candidature for an NVQ; however, they offer competence guidelines in other areas, including that of evaluation. The competence standards lead us to listing not only what should be performed in an occupation, but also the level required and the range of functions, most of which can be assessed with a minimum of subjectivity. The Standards not only consider the task and job description, but also the person specification in the same terms.

NVQs are awarded at different levels relating to the range of roles and tasks performed by the individual. The Training and Development Lead Body has developed three levels of NVQ – Levels 3, 4 and 5 – and the awarding bodies offer NVQs at these levels based on the Units of Competence. Each level requires that certain Units and parts of Units should be demonstrated by the candidate before an NVQ can be awarded. Units are awarded on a Unit by Unit basis until the required selection has been assessed for competence.

The NVQs determined by the 1994 review of Standards consist of Level 3 Training and Development, Level 4 Training and Development (Learning Development), Level 4 Training and Development (Human Resource Development) and Level 5 Training and Development. Each of these NVQs requires candidates to satisfy a Unit award in determined selections, which currently are:

- Level 3 Training and Development – 7 core plus 3 optional (from 12 options) Units.
- Level 4 Learning Support – 7 core and 5 (from 19) options.
- Level 4 Human Resource Development – 7 core plus 5 (from 19) options.
- Level 5 Training and Development – 7 core plus 5 (from 10) options.

Examples of requirements for two of these awards would be as follows.

Level 3 Training and Development NVQ

This NVQ will be sought by the majority of trainers with a principally direct training role. The Units required for the award of the NVQ consist of seven core Units that include such standards as:

A22 Identify individual learning needs.
B22 Design training and development sessions.
B33 Prepare and develop resources to support learning.
E23 Evaluate training and development sessions.
E31 Evaluate and develop own practice.

There are also three options to be taken from a list of 12, including such Standards as:

C22 Agree learning programmes with learners.
C24 Facilitate learning through demonstration and instruction.
C27 Facilitate group learning.
D32 Assess candidate performance.
D33 Assess candidate using diverse evidence.

Level 4 Training and Development (Learning) NVQ

This NVQ will be sought by the majority of trainers with not only a principally direct training role but one including wider functions and also a significant management function. Level 4 Training and Development (HRD) is similar, but with a rather more organizational influence. The Units required for the award of the Level 4 Training and Development (Learning) NVQ consist of seven core units, for example.

A21   Identify individuals' learning requirements.
B21   Design learning programmes to meet learners' requirements.
D11   Monitor and review progress with learners.
E21   Evaluate training and development programmes.
E31   Evaluate and develop own practice.

Five options are to be taken from a list of 19, including:

B31   Design, test and modify training and development materials.
B33   Prepare and develop resources to support learning.
D31   Design methods to collect evidence of competence performance.
D33   Assess candidates using diverse evidence.
D34   Support and verify the internal assessment process.

The Standards therefore appear to have significant value in the evaluation of training, development and learning and offer an almost ready-made instrument for this purpose. 'Almost' because the acceptance criterion for the Standards is simply whether the person can or cannot perform at the competency level defined – there are no graduations of skill beyond the ability to do. The most obvious use of the Standards in evaluation is in the definition of a person's knowledge and skills before and after the training programme, and this approach is increasingly being used. One example will be described later.

RESPONSIBILITY FOR EVALUATION

Everybody in the organization has their role to fulfil at some time and every encouragement must be given to them to do so, rather than stating that it is somebody else's problem or task.

THE TRAINING QUINTET

The ideal situation for an evaluation approach uses a range of role holders, and I describe this collection of people as the training quintet – senior managers, line managers, training manager, trainer and learner. For an effective approach, all members of this quintet must play their full part in all aspects of training. This enables much more to be included than if everything was laid on the shoulders of the trainer. Here we shall consider specifically their roles in evaluation. The training quintet format is summarized in Figure 2.3.

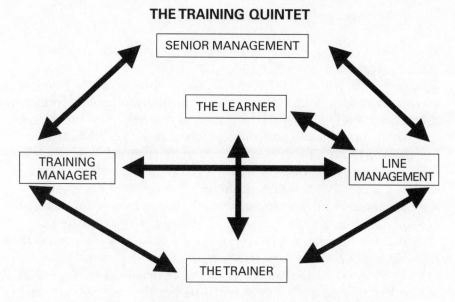

THE TRAINING QUINTET

Figure 2.3 *The training quintet*

Senior management

Although not directly involved in the performance of evaluation, senior management must play a significant part, principally by:

- authorizing resources to enable it to be carried out;
- taking an active part in requiring it to be done;
- taking an obvious, real and actively analytical interest in the results.

There is little value in training's principal clients and sponsors stating that they support the evaluation aspect of training without demonstrating this support in a practical manner. Such an approach would show only superficial interest. The roles of senior management in training and development are shown in Figure 2.4, evaluation roles being shown in open font italics.

- DEVELOP AND PUBLISH TRAINING STRATEGY
- ACTIVELY INVOLVE TRAINING FUNCTION AT EARLY PLANNING STAGES
- *REQUIRE EVALUATION TO BE PERFORMED*
- *EXAMINE AND DISCUSS EVALUATION RESULTS*

Figure 2.4 *Senior management roles in the training quintet*

The training manager

The training manager must be a moving force in the progress of evaluation of training *for which he or she has a responsibility.* This manager acts as the link between the senior manager clients and the trainers, and must also remind the trainers that evaluation is essential. Trainers can only too easily let this slip from their minds when they are caught up in the complexities and difficulties of the training itself. The training manager may have a network of trainers from whom sets of evaluation instruments arrive as the training year progresses. These *must* be analysed and collated so that meaningful reports can be prepared for senior management. The trainers should be encouraged to take an active interest in the progressive collation of the information they provide, and the training manager will want to hold discussions with the trainer group about what these collations show.

The trainers may need to be motivated to make a commitment to evaluation, to regard it as an essential part of the training cycle and not simply an enforced chore; the training manager is an essential part of this encouragement. Figure 2.5 summarizes the roles of the training manager in the training quintet.

■ AGREEING TRAINING PRINCIPLES AND PROGRAMMES
■ INVOLVEMENT AND LINKING WITH SENIOR MANAGEMENT
■ CONTROLLING EVALUATION POLICY AND PRACTICE
■ EXAMINING EVALUATION RESULTS
■ PREPARING EVALUATION REPORT FOR SENIOR MANAGEMENT

Figure 2.5 *Training manager roles in the training quintet*

The line manager

In most organizations the line manager is underused in the training and development area, and certainly in the evaluation process. Many line managers claim that they are already overloaded with work, without adding activities that many of them see as the province of the trainer. The simple response to these claims is that they cannot afford *not* to be involved. Whether or not they are making direct financial contributions to the training and development of their staff, training is costing them money – loss of a productive resource during the training period – and hence a devaluation of their department's production. Trained staff should provide effective production, and this costs money: does the line manager know what this cost is and whether value for money is being obtained?

There are three basic training and development activities in which line managers should be involved:

1. effective selection of the appropriate training programmes for their staff;
2. holding a pre-course briefing meeting with the learner;
3. holding a post-course debriefing meeting with the learner to identify learner-proposed action and resource assistance necessary.

But the value of the line manager's intervention should not stop at this and, if commitment is encouraged, they can be invaluable to the trainer, not only in supporting the training but also in what should be a natural process of direct involvement in the long-term evaluation. Some of these activities are suggested in Figure 2.6.

> - TRAINING NEEDS IDENTIFICATION
> - SELECTION OF STAFF FOR TRAINING
> - INVOLVEMENT IN TRAINING DESIGN
> - INVOLVEMENT IN TRAINING AND TRAINING SUPPORT
> - INVOLVEMENT IN EVALUATION DESIGN
> - PRE-COURSE BRIEFINGS
> - POST-COURSE DEBRIEFINGS
> - LEARNING IMPLEMENTATION SUPPORT
> - MEDIUM- AND LONG-TERM EVALUATION

Figure 2.6 *Line manager roles in the training quintet*

Trainers frequently complain about line managers' apparent lack of interest in the training programmes and any attempt to involve them in evaluation. If this is so (and so many cases are reported that it would seem to be the majority situation), positive attempts must be made to involve the line manager.

Although many trainers complain about the lack of interest, or of experiencing difficulties in getting managers to commit to fulfilling their responsibilities, one reason may be the traditionally protective attitude of trainers to anything that is linked to training. Organizations with good interrelationships between the training department and line management commonly involve line managers in training plans at the earliest opportunity – certainly at the planning and the content design stages. This involvement will ensure that the manager feels some ownership of, and hence commitment to, the training.

Similarly, when the evaluation approach is being planned, the line manager should be invited to contribute and, in so doing, with the accompanying commitment, can be encouraged to take a more active part, thus enabling more extensive evaluation. A specific instance of this is long-term evaluation, when the learner's implementation of planned action is being assessed. This leads on to the line manager's assessment of the cost-effective value of the training.

Line managers have always to be convinced of the value of their use of some of their time in what (again traditionally) is considered to be what trainers do. The benefits of mutual involvement are so great that a trainer's or training department plans must include a programme of activities to win over line management. Such a programme can include:

- invitations to line managers for their involvement in planning the training programme;
- invitations to line managers for their involvement in planning the evaluation process;
- visits to line managers to discuss training and evaluation and agree these involvements – an expensive approach with a large number of managers, but the eventual results will be well worth the expenditure;
- invitations to attend training courses as observers so that they can learn at first hand what happens to their staff;
- contributions by the trainers at meetings of line managers to describe what is happening in training; training plans and objectives; the desirable roles and responsibilities of different role holders; how the line manager can help training and how trainers can help line management; and so on;
- offers by trainers to give active support to the managers at different evaluation stages: for example, by accompanying the manager

when the medium- and long-term evaluations are being performed (although not taking over these functions);

■ workshops for line managers where discussions can take place and agreements made about roles and responsibilities.

The trainer

The direct and active involvement of the trainers in the evaluation of their programmes is an absolute necessity. Their principal roles in evaluation are summarized in Figure 2.7, but they are in the position to do the following:

■ support (as agreed) the line manager's pre-course activity with the learner – supply of *full* programme information, support for the pre-course briefing etc;

■ identify the knowledge and skill levels of their learners at the start of the programmes (unless this has taken place before the learner attends);

■ monitor the level and extent of learning as the programme continues;

■ modify the programme as an immediate result of the interim monitoring;

■ identify the knowledge and skill levels of the learners at the end of the programme;

■ steer the learners to the production of a post-training action plan;

■ undertake with the learners a validation of the training programme itself (and, in some instances, assessment of the trainers' performance);

■ support (as agreed) the line manager's post-course debriefing with the learner;

■ support (as agreed) the line manager's long-term evaluation of the implementation of the learning (this might be performed by the trainers themselves or their representatives so that not only is the learning evaluated, but a longer-term validation of the training can take place).

The learner

Finally, although the principal role of the learner in the programme is to learn, they must be involved in the evaluation process – essentially so, as without their comments much of the evaluation would not occur.

- *SUPPORTING LINE MANAGERS IN THEIR TRAINING NEEDS IDENTIFICATION AND TRAINING NEEDS ANALYSIS ROLES*
- *DESIGNING AND IMPLEMENTING PROGRAMME VALIDATION*
- *DESIGNING AND SUPPORTING OR IMPLEMENTING OVERALL EVALUATION*
- *SUPPORTING LINE MANAGERS IN THEIR BRIEFING AND DEBRIEFING ROLES*
- *SUPPORTING LINE MANAGERS IN THEIR MEDIUM- AND LONG-TERM EVALUATION ROLES*

Figure 2.7 *Trainer roles in the training quintet*

In order to assist in the evaluation they must be committed to completing any assessment instruments honestly and in full, avoiding (as far as is humanly possible!) contamination of their comments by euphoric or negative feelings. They must not be allowed to feel that they are completing a paper-chase or number-crunching exercise, but be made aware of exactly why they are being asked to do certain things, what they will be used for, and with whom. This type of knowledge will help to ensure that meaningful and realistic comments are made. The principal roles of the learner in training and evaluation (excluding their participation) are summarized in Figure 2.8.

- INVOLVEMENT IN THE PLANNING AND DESIGN OF THE TRAINING PROGRAMME
- *INVOLVEMENT IN THE PLANNING AND DESIGN OF THE EVALUATION PROCESS*
- *INTEREST IN AND SUPPORT OF THE EVALUATION APPROACHES*

Figure 2.8 *Learner roles in the training quintet*

One common omission in evaluation programmes is a failure to let the learners know the results of their support. Evaluation questionnaires appear, are completed by the learners, then disappear never to be heard of or seen by them again, until perhaps magically produced at subsequent meetings and used against them! If the results are to be used in subsequent evaluation activities, let the learners know this, and seek their advice on how the information might be used most effectively.

If this culture is induced in an organization among senior, training and line managers, and among trainers and learners, not only will the evaluation be more effective as a result, but the training and development will also be more effective, and seen as valuable throughout the organization. The development of this supportive culture will not happen overnight in organizations where it does not already exist, nor will it develop without committed work by, usually, the trainers and their training manager. The claim by line managers of lack of time is often well founded and the apparent lack of interest by senior management frequently exists only because of ignorance of their role, or perhaps relegation of the process through non-understanding of the reason for and value of evaluation. A programme of education should be embarked upon, preferably on all fronts at the same time, otherwise one element might negate the agreed intentions of others.

3

Before the Training and Development Programme

THE EVALUATION MODEL

The evaluation model was introduced in Chapter 2 and the remainder of this book will be related to that model wherever relevant. The model is repeated in Figure 3.1.

1. Training needs analysis leading to training objectives
2. Design of the evaluation process
3. Pre-course testing or assessment of knowledge, skills and attitudes
4. Line manager pre-course briefing
5. Interim assessment and validation
6. End of programme testing
7. End of programme reaction review
8. End of programme validation
9. Learner action planning
10. Line manager post-course debriefing
11. Medium-term follow up
12. Long-term follow up
13. Cost and value effectiveness analysis
14. Assessment and report on achievement of the objectives

Figure 3.1 *The evaluation model*

This chapter will be concerned with stages 1 to 4.

TRAINING NEEDS ANALYSIS

The processes of effective training needs identification and analysis are too complex and extensive to be covered here, and are dealt with most satisfactorily in a number of other publications, some of which are referred to in the recommended reading list. Suffice it to say that before any aspect of training and development and evaluation is considered, a training needs analysis must be undertaken to determine that:

- the training subject is really needed;
- it is clear whether the proposed training is introductory or remedial;
- the people involved are in need of training;
- everything is known about the subject for which training has been decided;
- the extent of existing knowledge or skill among the potential target population has been considered.

As a result of the consolidation of such information, the business of developing the training programme can commence. Areas to be considered include:

- What extent of material will need to be included?
- What will be the most effective form of training – a course, open learning, mentoring, one-to-one instruction, literature research etc?
- What forms of practical activities should be included, to what extent, and where in the programme?
- How long will the programme take to complete?
- How many trainers/guests will be required (if a training course)?
- How will an open learning programme be supported?
- Where will the training or learning take place?

The final questions to be considered once the training has been designed (or parallel with its design) are:

- What form should the evaluation take?
- How much time and resource will be available for evaluation?
- When will it need to be performed?
- Who will be responsible for (a) designing it, (b) administering it and (c) analysing and reporting?
- Who will need to see and/or what will be done with the results?

An absolute essential for *any* training programme must be the determination of the terminal objectives sought from the programme, objectives stated comprehensively and unequivocally, and in terms of time allowances, standards sought, tolerances allowed and so on. Any effective form of evaluation demands these objectives, otherwise the evaluators will not know what they are evaluating and which measures will show in the evaluation whether the training and learning have been successful.

It is only when this information is available from the post-TNA design of the training programme that an evaluation format can even be considered. How true to current, real life are these requirements? In my experience there are only limited cases where this approach is followed, although with the introduction of NVQs and Investors in People, and an increasing awareness of the value of evaluation, these are growing in quantity and quality. But I believe there is a long way to go, as the views of many trainers and managers is still that evaluation equals the completion of the 'happiness' sheet in the last five minutes of a training course. If you remain unconvinced about evaluation, re-read pages 5–14 on the benefits of evaluation and the consequences of not doing it.

In training and development the starting and finishing points are the setting and achieving of objectives: evaluation is inexorably linked to these and, in fact, extends them by continuing beyond the training and into the areas of the implementation of learning in the workplace. In these ways the initial training needs identifications and analyses can be justified and validated.

DESIGN OF THE EVALUATION PROCESS

It is difficult to quote a golden rule for the design of evaluation measures, other than that the evaluation format must be congruent with the type of training and development to be evaluated. Too often one form of evaluation is used for every different kind of learning process offered, whether it is relevant or not. Usually the evaluation form in these cases is neither useful nor valid.

The basic principle behind any evaluation design is that the process must approach the training and learning objectives with a view to confirming whether or not they have been achieved, and subsequently implemented in an effective manner. This overall requirement includes the validation of the actual training process itself:

- Was it the most appropriate method?
- Was it presented in the most effective way?
- Did it support the learners and help them to learn?
- Were the training objectives achieved?

It also covers factors relating to the learners:

- Were their starting and finishing levels identified and assessed in some way?
- Were their personal objectives satisfied as far as they correlated with those of the programme?
- Was the learning method the most appropriate for them?
- To what extent did they learn or not learn (and why)?
- What do they intend to do with the learning and, eventually, did they do it?

In order to obtain answers to these and other questions, it will obviously be necessary to identify the learning change of the learners and, frequently, get feedback from them about the quality and value to them of the training process. The maximum possible information needs to be obtained from them about their learning, in terms of:

- What have they learned?
- How has this happened?
- What do they intend to do with the learning?
- If they did not learn as much as you/they would have wished, why not?

These are the essentials in the evaluation feedback approaches, although at times it will be necessary to seek other information, views and opinions in the form of the participants' reactions to certain aspects – the form of the training programme, its length, the most and least useful aspects, sessions and activities, the level of the training facilities and so on.

The former type of feedback sought is *validation* and the latter *reaction*; validation is essential in terms of the actual training and learning, whereas reaction must be a secondary aspect which, although contributing something to the learning, has not the same vital nature.

Design of the evaluation must take account of both these approaches and, if both are required, arrangements made for the collection of both types of information and views.

DESIGNING VARIED FORMS OF EVALUATION

Consideration of the form of the training will indicate fairly readily the type and extent of evaluation measures, but in general they will look at whether to include:

- pre-testing or pre-knowledge measures of the learners' existing skills and knowledge;
- start of course assessments either replacing pre-programme assessments or confirming these in more training-specific forms;
- daily or interval interim evaluation approaches – these will normally only be considered if the learning programme extends over more than a day or so, but will certainly be necessary in programmes with a duration of a week or more;
- end of programme evaluation and/or reaction and allied activities;
- the form of action planning and plans for its use;
- arrangements for medium- and long-term evaluation, either by correspondence or visiting, and by whom.

Equally essential in the planning and design stage will be the confirmation of arrangements with people other than the training staff who are likely to be or should be involved in the evaluation process – the training quintet – and their various responsibilities. At this stage the people responsible for the evaluation should ensure that the quintet is fully aware of their responsibilities and are taking or will take action in accord with these. This contact will be particularly important with the learners' line managers to ensure support in general in addition to pre-course briefing and post-course debriefing, with all that these involve.

Figure 3.2 gives a series of minimum guidelines to ensure that you have followed all the evaluation planning and design steps necessary, at the time that the training itself is being planned – not half-way through the training, nor at the end or after the event when you realize that you should have evaluated (or someone in the quintet asks you for the results of your evaluation!).

THE LINE MANAGER'S INVOLVEMENT

Of paramount importance in any evaluation programme and process is the active involvement of the learners' line managers. It is they who will (should) have been involved in the training needs analyses and

---

1. Has a training needs analysis been performed?
2. What are the objectives for the training event?
3. Do the objectives lend themselves to being evaluated? If not, why not and what else could be done?
4. Confirm line management support action.
5. Decide the timing, resourcing and extent of the evaluation process you need to follow.
6. Are you concentrating on full validation or merely reaction?
7. Create instruments that will satisfy your evaluation needs.
8. If possible, test your evaluative instruments against the training programme items.
9. Decide on the form of end of programme action planning.
10. Agree post-programme evaluation action – who, what, where, when?

Figure 3.2 *A checklist for evaluation pre-planning*

have agreed that their staff should be given the opportunity to learn new skills or procedures, or to undertake remedial training to bring them up to the required competence standards. This agreement places on them a requirement of involvement and does not absolve them from any further action. On too many occasions, once training has been agreed, the line manager, for sometimes justifiable reasons, says 'this is now the province of the training or HRD department; over to you'. The manager should not be allowed to 'get away with this', and if the culture of the organization is right, the training department will have obtained the manager's commitment to support and involvement. Line managers are busy people, usually in a difficult, in-between position, and every attempt should be made within the organization to obtain their commitment. In theory this should be relatively easy, as the more involvement line managers have in the development of their staff the greater likelihood there will be of a successful learning conclusion, with improved skills, efficiency and attitudes, and more effective working as a result.

Two specific activities can be described at this stage: the pre-programme briefing meeting, and the post-programme debriefing meeting.

Pre-programme briefing meetings

This is a vital process in the development of people who are to take part in training and development provided by other than the line managers themselves. The dialogue between a line manager and his or her staff will have started some time before the training programme is due – training needs will have been identified at an appraisal or other career development discussion, or will have come about as a result of the introduction of new tasks or roles. The need for training or development will have been agreed, and someone will have taken the necessary action to identify the relevant and appropriate training programme and made arrangements for the individuals to enter these programmes.

Preferably within the fortnight prior to the start of the training programme the line manager should invite the learner to a pre-course briefing discussion. This will be a last-minute opportunity to confirm the training or agree on its cancellation, and will also be an opportunity for the two to discuss it, along with the hopes and aspirations of both. The line manager should ensure that there is sufficient time for a meaningful discussion to take place, particularly if the learner has concerns or fears that need to be allayed. The learner might have prepared by considering the programme objectives and content and identifying his or her own objectives. Because they are two individuals, one responsible for the other, it is likely that their views of needs and objectives may differ slightly: this is the opportunity for both to discover these differences and agree common objectives. The meeting is important, but need not be over-long since, if the relationship between the manager and staff is good, there should be little in the way of surprises.

With the responsibilities of the training quintet in mind, the line manager can usefully pass on significant information to the trainers that will help a learner on the training programme. This information can be used to modify the material to be included in the programme, particularly if a number of managers report on the same subject. Unfortunately this occurs only too rarely, but it is an ideal occasion for co-operation and the development of relationships between the trainers and the line managers.

Probably the worst scenario in manager–staff relationships, unless completely unavoidable, would be for the learner to disappear to the learning programme with no contact with the line manager, drawing the obvious conclusion that the manager is not interested in the individual's development.

Figure 3.3 suggests some guidelines to help the line manager make the pre-programme briefing meaningful. It can be helpful if the learner sees this list in advance to help in *their* preparation for the discussion.

The questions you should be considering at the pre-programme briefing meeting with the learner include:

1. As the training is a need for development of the learner, has there been any significant change since the event was agreed?
2. Is this course or event the most relevant one to satisfy the learner's needs?
3. Discuss with the learner the programme objectives as far as your local organization is concerned, ie the office, the section, the team etc.
4. Discuss with the learner the programme objectives as far as it affects the learner – at what level of skill and knowledge does the learner see him/herself at this pre-programme stage?
5. Discuss how the learner will approach the training – specific areas for emphasis, personal disclosure, etc.
6. Any other aspects not covered by the above.
7. Give guarantee of managerial support when the learner returns.
8. Agree a date and time for a post-programme debriefing meeting (to be held soon after the training event).

Figure 3.3 *Pre-programme briefing checklist*

Post-programme debriefing meetings

Although this stage is out of chronological order it has such strong links with the pre-programme briefing meeting that it is useful to consider them together. The post-programme meeting is even more important than the pre-course one, as it is from this that the learner and manager start to implement the learning achieved and the action plans made. The meeting should be held as soon as possible after the learner's completion of the programme, certainly within a week. Failure to do this will suggest to the learner that their completion of the training is considered of little value, with the result that, unless they are very committed, the action plans will not be implemented.

Figure 3.4 suggests guidelines for this meeting, perhaps the most important aspect being the agreement by the line manager to support as actively as required the learner's implementation plans. It should be made clear that this meeting does not wipe the manager's hands of the process but, with arrangements for at least one further review, it is the start of the implementation process.

The questions you should be considering at the post-course debriefing meeting with the learner include:

1. How effective was the training programme as far as the learner was personally concerned? Did this differ from the views of others?
2. How effective were the trainers? Approachable, logical, clear in their presentations, good use of visual aids, not too hurried etc?
3. How appropriate was the training material as far as the learner was concerned?
4. How up to date was the material?
5. Were the programme objectives achieved? If not, why not?
6. Were the learner's personal objectives achieved? If not, why not?
7. What did the learner learn as new material, have usefully confirmed or be timeously reminded of?
8. Discuss with the learner their action plan:
   What is planned?   How is it to be implemented?
   When and over what period?   What resources are required?
   Can you help/does the learner want you to help in any way?
9. Any other aspects not covered by the above.
10. Arrange a date, between three and six months hence, to discuss with the learner a final implementation review. Offer interim reviews.
11. Discuss with the relevant trainers any feedback information about which you feel they should be aware.

Figure 3.4 *Post-programme debriefing checklist*

This list of questions and subjects to raise should allay one of the fears expressed by line managers about the post-programme meetings, namely what should be discussed. Obviously there are almost innumerable subjects and with some pre-planning by the manager, and the learner, the meeting can be a significant occasion during which learner–manager relationships can be improved or consolidated.

On occasions the discussion can raise questions, the solutions to which may either not be clear to the learner or the manager, or may suggest that further training is required. In such cases the *trainers* should be prepared to assist with the discussion, offering their knowledge and expertise.

With the responsibilities of the training quintet again in mind, the manager should certainly feed back to the trainers any information about the training programme that emerges from the discussion (with the agreement of the learner). Too rarely does feedback of this nature reach the trainers in this way, yet the learner may feel able to speak more freely to the manager than directly to the trainers.

4

—

The Construction of Tests – I

A variety of tests can be found at all stages of evaluation, but are more usually encountered:

- prior to the training and development programme;
- at the start of the programme;
- progressively during a programme;
- at the end of the event.

Their contributions to training are demonstrated in Figure 4.1.

1. AN ASSESSMENT OF THE KNOWLEDGE, SKILLS AND ATTITUDES LEVELS PRIOR TO THE TRAINING
2. MEASUREMENT OF LEARNING OVER THE PERIOD OF THE PROGRAMME
3. SUPPORTING FEEDBACK TO LEARNERS DURING AN EVENT
4. FEEDBACK TO THE TRAINERS OR OTHER PROGRAMME PRODUCERS ON THE EFFECTIVENESS OF THE TRAINING PROGRAMME.

Figure 4.1 *The contribution of testing to training*

Contribution 1 must be the most important of these, since it is essential to know from where the learners are coming if there is to be any form of evaluation to assess change itself and the amount of change. Tests of this nature can be administered before the learner takes part in the programme, but the tests must be correctly introduced to the learner.

This is much easier when the tests are used at the start of the training, but pre-testing does not take up training time.

A pre-programme or start of programme test does not *have* to be administered in every case – a point not made frequently enough. Pre-tests are set to determine the existing level of the learners. If this is known to be zero, then there is no need to set a test.

- *If the equipment, knowledge, procedure or skill is completely new, then there would be only negative value in testing the learners at the start of the programme – the results would be 'failure', and the learners would be asking 'what was the use of setting that?'*

Testing during an event, Contribution 2, is particularly important during a complex and/or lengthy programme. The results of the tests give the learners and the trainers effective, immediate feedback on the success of the event, and whether there needs to be any modification of training or learning. The frequency of formal tests must be considered seriously, as too frequent testing can become annoying to the learners, with negative results. Tests have an inherent problem in that, for adults, they are too easily associated with bad memories of interminable tests at school, usually for punitive reasons. This concept must be studiously avoided in adult learning, and in many cases the test can be disguised by having the learners perform a natural task during the programme, the results of which are equivalent to a formal test.

Contribution 3 is very similar to 2, but involves feeding back to the learners the results of the tests. This is probably the most difficult and dangerous part of the testing process. As suggested above, the feedback may be seen as punitive or as 'putting down' the learners, obviously something to be avoided at all costs. On too many occasions the tester considers that posting the group results in a form of league table will give the learners maximum information. No doubt it does, and the learners at the top end of the table will have a 'feel good' factor, but what about the ones at the bottom of the table – how will they feel about their placements being publicly displayed? If comparative results have to be used, if at all possible, comment should be made to individuals.

Finally, Contribution 4 is an essential part of the validation and evaluation process, as essential as the start of training testing. Little is achieved if there is initial testing but nothing at the end of the programme. The two tests demonstrate the change over the programme, ie the effectiveness of both the learning and the training. A difficult, although not impossible feature, is the repetitive nature of the tests.

There will be little opportunity for valid assessment if the test at the end does not relate to the initial test – if it is different, how can the results be compared and change identified? The ideal way for you to achieve this is to use the same test at the start of the programme and at the end.

DESIGNING TESTS

Specific guidelines for the design and construction of particular tests will be found on pages 49–66, but the guidelines suggested here apply to the majority of knowledge tests.

Test design can be considered in nine stages, following a logical progression.

Stage 1

The initial action, having decided that a test or tests should be used, is to decide where in the course, programme etc it should be used. As suggested at the start of the chapter this can be at either, some or all of the following:

- prior to the training and development programme;
- at the start of the programme;
- progressively during a programme;
- at the end of the event.

Part of the consideration, particularly for tests that might be used progressively during the programme, will be to ensure that there is not a test overload – you can so easily become obsessed with the value and use of tests that you include too many. There is always the danger that the learners will become anti-test in such circumstances, and a lot of valid information will be lost.

Stage 2

With the objectives of the session or programme in mind, select the most important topics; this selection will suggest the essential coverage for your tests. Your selection obviously requires that you not only have effective objectives for the session etc, and may require you to reconsider these objectives. If any of the objectives do not include the elements of effective objectives – for example, the standard to be reached is not stated clearly, it will be impossible to design a test for this area.

Stage 3

Bearing in mind the nature of the material with which the test(s) will be used, you will now need to decide on the type of test that will be most appropriate. Descriptions of the principal types of knowledge tests are contained in the remainder of this chapter and practical tests in the following chapter. These should help you to make your selections. Be careful not to select on the basis of ease of use or personal preference, but more on complete relevance of the test to the subject.

Stage 4

Having selected the format or type of test(s) to be used, a start on the construction of the test can now be made. Follow the guidelines and other advice in the descriptions of the specific tests, and produce a provisional test. One common mistake made at this stage is to leave too little time for test construction, either for sufficient consideration or too close to the event, with the result that it is rushed.

Once the draft has been made, try it out on colleagues or other people who could at some time be participants in the training programme. There should by now be no problem over the relevance of the content of the test, but the 'dummy run(s)' should ensure that the test questions are clear and intelligible, and the test instructions equally clear. The practice tests should be assessed in the same way that the real test would be to ensure that the analysis demonstrates what you intended it to show.

If the test is to be used on a number of programmes, confirmation of the test's validity will also enable it to be used on successive programmes, so ensuring consistency of evaluation.

Stage 5

A final check for valid use should be made to ensure that, although your control group understood the test, other heterogeneous groups would also understand it. The language – ethic, colloquial, jargonistic or its complexity – can affect this understanding, and every attempt should be made to ensure a universal level if the test is to be used on a number of occasions. The aim is not to demonstrate how clever you are at constructing tests, but to produce tests that can be easily understood. Avoid 'clever' language and aim for words and phrases that are as clear, plain and simple as possible within the context of the training. Remember the objective of the examination is to test *what* the learners know, not how clever they are linguistically or at solving linguistic puzzles.

Stage 6

Decide how the learners will be required to answer the test questions. The usual alternatives include the following.

Exclusion method

In this method, if alternatives are offered, the incorrect response has to be struck through. For example, if the learners have to choose between 'Yes/No', the response choices are entered in this way. If the chosen correct response is 'No', a stroke should be placed through 'Yes'.

Marking method

Again, if alternatives are offered, this is usually as a list or with separated space (for example 'Yes   No'). The correct response would be circled.

Boxing

This method is usually encountered when there are several possible responses offered, as in the multi-choice test. A small box can be placed against each possible response in which the learner places a tick or cross to indicate their preferred choice. If you use this method, make it very clear in the instructions *how* the choice should be indicated (and be prepared for this instruction to be ignored!).

Separate text

With some tests – for example, the essay – the responses need to be written on separate sheets. Ensure that these are available and, if they are to be used for several questions, divided in an appropriate manner.

Stage 7

Write the instructions for completing the test and include them with the test. The most appropriate place for them is at the start of the test or at the start of each question if the method of responses varies from one question to another. The method of response, as described in Stage 6, should be clearly indicated – ticks, crosses, strokes, circling, box entries etc – particularly on each occasion that a change of response method occurs.

Stage 8

Construct a scoring key. This may seem unimportant if the trainer who sets the test is the only one who will be analysing the results, but it may sometimes be necessary for others, who may not be acquainted with the test, to perform the scoring and analysis. Scoring of the essay test will be the most difficult, but the basic criterion must be, not to test academic excellence in writing essays, but to ensure that the relevant answers are contained. A list of required answers to be included and identified will be helpful for the scorer.

Stage 9

Decide on and construct some form of summary analysis on which the results of each member of a group can be entered for each test performed. This results in a permanent record demonstrating the progression of the learners throughout an event and helps towards recognition of validation of the training. The summary analysis can be in matrix form and usually only needs to be in a simple format. Figure 4.2 suggests a typical format. The entries in the columns for the range of tests should be consistently presented, and the most useful format is the results converted into percentages of 'correct' answers – this enables comparisons to be made between dissimilar numbers of results.

NAMES OF LEARNERS/ NAMES OF TESTS	1	2	3	4
A	66%	70%	83%	98%
B	43%	63%	75%	92%
C	68%	71%	80%	96%
D	61%	76%	81%	99%
etc				

Figure 4.2 *A matrix record for progressive tests*

TYPES OF TESTS

The various tests and their methods of construction will be described in this section, as they are related principally to the start of the programme, although as will be seen they are commonly repeated at other stages.

A variety of tests exists, and it is essential that you select the appropriate form of test for a particular event, otherwise the results will scarcely be valid. As suggested above, a test need not be a formal, sit down and write form of test, but can be introduced in such a way that the learners do not realize they are being tested. Tests can be of:

- knowledge – not always, but usually, written;
- skills – either operating, procedural or more general skills; usually practical, and which can be preceded by a written knowledge skill;
- attitudes and behaviour – usually practical, observational approaches.

This section will concentrate on tests of knowledge. Although it is not essential, these are usually in the form of a written test and may precede a practical test of skill so that all aspects of learning are covered.

KNOWLEDGE TESTS

Tests of knowledge are the more common forms of formal tests, and are usually written, but they certainly suffer from the potential problems described above. However, provided they are constructed effectively, they are objective, usually simple to administer and form a permanent record of achievement (or lack of it). The principal expenditure of time is in their construction and marking – both resource time as, ideally, the tests themselves should be reasonably short, requiring a minimum of time from the learners. Some guidelines for their construction are summarized in Figure 4.3.

TEST QUESTIONS

Tests of knowledge will normally consist of a written questionnaire of some kind, requiring written responses. The discipline of psychology requires the questions to be posed in accordance with a number of set rules to ensure fairness, consistency and validity. Although not decrying this discipline, few test constructors (who are usually practising

- Do you really need to introduce this test?
- Do you have firm, comprehensive and measurable training objectives?
- Are the test questions related directly to the objectives and only to subjects included in the programme?
- Do not try to include questions about everything in the programme unless it is a very limited one – select the most important or significant aspects.
- Design the test in the most appropriate format – this could include a sequential order of questions, depending on whether the test is at the start or the finish.
- The instructions for completing the test must be accurate and comprehensive, eg whether ticks, circles, textual answers etc are required.
- 'Test' the test with non-training groups before going live to highlight any snags or inaccuracies.
- Keep records of the test results to assess validity – widely differing results will suggest an invalid test.

Figure 4.3 *Guidelines for test construction*

trainers) are aware of these rules and may not have the time or opportunity to study them. However, if a fairly simple set of guidelines is followed, as summarized below, gross errors should not occur and the test should give the trainer sufficient information.

1. Include questions that refer to subjects, topics or aspects covered by the training only – trick questions outside this range can only devalue the test, both in the minds of the learners and in its absolute validity.
2. Bearing in mind that the longer the test the less likely is the learner to take the test seriously, include sufficient questions to show whether or not learning is necessary or has been achieved. Guidance to this will be obtained from the specific objectives for the programme. If it is necessary to introduce a lengthy test questionnaire, vary the form of the questions. Shorter questionnaires can, of course, follow a completely internally consistent format.
3. Ensure that the language used will be completely understandable to the learners being tested and that the questions are clear and unambiguous. This is particularly important when the test is at the start of the programme, before 'technical' terms have been

introduced. Of course, the use of these terms may be part of the initial test to assess the scale of the learner's existing knowledge. Ask yourself, are the questions worded

- as simply as possible;
- as briefly as possible;
- as directly as possible;
- unambiguously for the group?

4. Pose the question in such a way that it gives no clues about the answer to that question, or to following questions. Ask yourself, do the questions
   - involve one idea only;
   - influence the response in any way;
   - avoid leading the response;
   - avoid influencing each other?
5. Use positive forms of questions rather than ones including a negative.
6. Do not include 'trick' questions – these can reduce the credibility of the test. The only exception of which I am aware that I feel is justifiable is the questionnaire that asks a number of questions, the last of which is an instruction to answer only the first question – this reinforces guidance to learners to read *everything* through before starting work.
7. When response choices are listed, ensure that the 'correct' response falls in different positions of the list for each question.
8. Each question should normally have only one correct answer, unless opinions are being sought.
9. Ensure that the test can be completed in the time allocated – pre-testing of the test can help in assessing the time necessary for 'average' learners.

FORMS OF TESTS OF KNOWLEDGE

Figure 4.4 summarizes the principal forms of knowledge test in use.

- ■ ESSAYS
- ■ SHORT ANSWER
- ■ BINARY CHOICE
- ■ MULTIPLE CHOICE
- ■ MATCHING CHOICE
- ■ LIKERT THURSTONE SCALES
- ■ RANKING SCALES

Figure 4.4 *Principal forms of knowledge tests*

ESSAYS

These are principally used to test broad areas of knowledge and the learners' ability to construct effective responses from identified and analysed data or information. Abilities of interpretation cover particularly complex ideas or information, analysis, explanation, comparison, logical argument and presentation.

- The *advantages* include a demonstration of the abilities mentioned above.
- The *disadvantages* include the time taken to write the essay; a requirement to write clearly and at speed; the understanding of a common language among the learners; advantages to 'good' essay writers.

Guidelines

Figure 4.5 summarizes guidelines for constructing essay tests.

- Ensure that the subject required in the response is clearly defined
- Full instructions may be included about:
  - the length of response required
  - the time available
  - practical aspects of use of paper (both sides?)
- How the essay will be assessed

Figure 4.5 *Guidelines for essay construction*

The problems encountered by the test assessor will include:

- assessing an essay that does not follow the instructions completely;
- understanding some of the language used;
- comparing one essay with another;
- being a full expert on the subject;
- accepting that an essay is a less objective form of response than many of the other types.

SHORT-ANSWER TESTS

These are very similar to the essay, but require the learners to summarize, tabulate or make graphical representations of their responses rather than write lengthy, continuous, grammatical text. They may be required to list a number of items sought by the question; put an activity into sequential steps; summarize the advantages or disadvantages of an approach; and so on.

The short answer is less subjective than the essay, although many aspects of subjectivity still remain.

Guidelines

These are summarized in Figure 4.6.

- Check that the questions can in fact be answered by short answers
- Use direct questions in as brief and as clear a form as possible
- Use questions that are singular and require a singular response only
- Use the method for which short answers are possible
- Pose the questions so that non-essential words need not be used, eg 'a', 'an', 'some'
- Avoid a form of question that gives a clue to the response
- Avoid negatives as far as possible

Figure 4.6 *Guidelines for short-answer test construction*

BINARY CHOICE TESTS

This form of test is very objective and can be directly and clearly related to the objectives and the learning points of the programme. As the name implies, the learner is given the choice between two answers to the questions posed and consequently a large number of questions can be answered in a short period of time. Time needed for analysis of the responses is obviously reduced as the assessor only requires a checklist, against which the singular response is compared for correctness or incorrectness – consequently the marking need not be performed by the trainer or administrator.

Three major forms of the binary test in common use are:

1. Yes/No responses;
2. True/False responses;
3. Alternative responses.

Yes/No responses

An example of this, using the closed question approach, might be:

(Put a stroke through the one that does not apply.)

Does your company offer annual job appraisal reviews?   Yes/No

If so, are they offered to all staff?   Yes/No

Or:

(Circle the response you feel applies.)

Does your company offer annual job appraisal reviews?   Yes   No

If so, are they offered to all staff?   Yes   No

True/False responses

These are similar to Yes/No choices, but offer alternatives of the true or false response. They are usually posed in the form of a statement rather than a question. An example of this type of test might be:

(Put a stroke through the response that does not apply.)

The machine operator only is allowed to press the
stop button.   True/False

Or:

(Circle the response you feel applies.)

The machine operator only is allowed to press the
stop button.   True   False

Alternative responses

These are closer to the Yes/No response test than the True/False, as the responses answer a question. An example of this type of test might be:

> To whom would you look for   Your boss/Your boss's boss
> your annual appraisal interview?

Or:

> To whom would you look for   Your boss   Your boss's boss
> your annual appraisal interview?

The alternatives shown above demonstrate two of the common ways of having the learner answer the test. The correct answer from alternatives separated by a '/' can be shown by deleting the incorrect answer; where the responses are spaced, the correct answer can be ringed. Whichever method is used, it must be made clear what is required.

Guidelines

Guidelines for the construction of binary tests include those listed in Figure 4.7.

- Make the question or statement clear, unambiguous and as short as possible
- Ask only one question in each item
- Ensure that, say in a true/false situation, the statement is in fact one or the other
- Avoid as far as possible implied answers or value judgements in the question or statement
- Use negatives sparingly and avoid the use of 'every', 'never', 'always', as there are few situations that are invariably true or false
- Avoid the use of words like 'frequently', 'usually', 'may', 'quite' and 'sometimes', as these words can have different connotations to different people
- Make sure that the statement is sufficiently plausible not to appear obviously true or false

---

Figure 4.7 *Guidelines for binary test construction*

MULTIPLE-CHOICE TESTS

Multiple-choice tests are similar to binary tests but offer several alternative responses from which the learner chooses one. In some, more subjective situations, the 'correct' answer need not be absolutely correct, but will be the option that is appreciably more acceptable than the others. In this case you should be prepared for discussion when the tests are marked as some learners may not agree (with well-justified arguments) with the more acceptable answer.

There are two major forms of this type of test – the incomplete answer (as described in the binary choice test) and the offer of alternative responses.

The incomplete answer

An example of the incomplete answer test might be:

1. The person responsible for conducting your job appraisal review is:

    a) Your boss?
    b) Your boss's boss?
    c) An even more senior manager?
    d) A peer?
    e) A subordinate?
    f) None of the above (state whom)?

The learner is asked in the instructions for the test to tick or ring the correct answer.

Alternative response test

An example of the pure, alternative response test could be:

1. What are the recommended tyre pressures for a Zucat 327?

    a) $26lb/in^2$ front and rear ....? Please tick
    b) $28lb/in^2$ front and rear ....? the correct
    c) $28lb/in^2$ front, $30lb/in^2$ rear ....? answer
    d) $30lb/in^2$ front, $28lb/in^2$ rear ....?
    e) $40lb/in^2$ front and rear ....?

Guidelines

Guidelines to the construction of multiple-choice tests are very similar to those for binary tests, but also include those shown in Figure 4.8.

- Avoid giving clues to the correct answer; this often happens by making the correct answer obvious in some way – by the way it is expressed, or by making it longer than the others
- Vary the position in the list of the correct answer
- Number each question, but use letters – upper or lower case, followed by ')' – before each alternative to avoid numerical confusion in the answer
- Commence each alternative with an upper-case letter; close each with a question mark
- Do not include negatives in the stem
- Incorrect alternatives (distractors) should be plausible

Figure 4.8 *Guidelines for multiple-choice test construction*

MATCHING CHOICE TESTS

These tests consist of two sets or columns of elements, those in one column to be matched with those in the other column. This test version offers many possible variations with the use of words, letters, numbers, symbols, pictures etc.

An example of such a test could be:

Match the ranks with the service, entering the number of the appropriate service in the box after the rank.

Ranks		Service
a) Corporal	☐	1) Royal Navy
b) Stoker	☐	2) Army
c) Wing Commander	☐	3) Army
d) Torpedoman	☐	4) Royal Air Force
e) Guardsman	☐	5) Royal Navy

LIKERT AND THURSTONE SCALES

These are two specific approaches to binary and multiple-choice tests, each having an especial place in a particular learning situation. Both scales present the individual with a number of statements related to the training event, frequently at the subjective level, and require either agreement or disagreement with each statement. One variation offers a simple 'agree' or 'disagree' rating, as in the binary test, the other gives a wider range of agreement/disagreement, the latter avoiding polarized extremes of choice.

The Thurstone Scale

The Thurstone Scale requires responses of either A = you agree, or agree more than you disagree; or D = you disagree, or disagree more than you agree.

I.	A manager's first responsibility is the care of their staff.	D	A
2.	A manager must be able to do all the jobs of their staff.	D	A
3.	Managers are closer to their staff than their own boss.	D	A

The Likert Scale

The Likert Scale offers a wider variety of answers than the Thurstone Scale, thus avoiding the polarization criticism, and normally offers a range of five choices:

SA = Strongly agree   A = Agree more than you disagree
U = Uncertain
D = Disagree more than you agree   SD = Strongly disagree

An example of this scale, using the previous questioning, might be:

I	A manager's first responsibility is the care of their staff.	SA	A	U	D	SD
2	A manager must be able to do all the jobs of their staff.	SA	A	U	D	SD
3	Managers are closer to their staff that their own boss.	SA	A	U	D	SD

RANKING SCALES

In these scales polarized decisions are not involved, and the approach is particularly useful for encouraging the emergence of views, attitudes and learning without making this too obvious. The scale is particularly susceptible to manipulation, however, if the learners have read the 'right books' and the trainer/administrator must be prepared to discuss the results which, if the test is administered at the start of the training, may not be accepted by the learners.

The learners are required to place a number of statements in order of priority or importance, commencing with ranking 1. Without any external influences, these rankings should represent the views of the learner at, say, the start of the programme. Subsequent completion will show, by comparing the rankings, what changes have taken place during the learning programme (note that any change does not necessarily have to be due to the training – the change may be purely coincidental or reliant on other effects).

A typical ranking scale may be used on a management skills programme and could be as follows.

Good Management

The following are aspects of good management. Please rank them in order of their importance as far as *you* are concerned at this stage. Rank them in order according to how you actually feel, rather than how you think the trainer would like you to rank them. Put a '1' against the statement you feel is the most important; '2' against the next important and so on. Rank all the items. If you cannot decide at all which of two items rank higher than the other, give both equal ranking and rank the next statement at its real numerical position. For example, if two items fall at rank 5, both are ranked 5 (or alternatively 5.5) with the next statement at 7; if three items fall at 5, each are ranked at 5 with the next item at 8.

Item	Ranking
Support for their subordinates	....
Loyalty to the organization	....
Coaching their subordinates	....
Making training opportunities available	....

and so on.

5

The Construction of Tests – 2

Training and development programmes designed to achieve the learning of knowledge alone are rare nowadays because of the enlightened approach to learning in that knowledge without practical or practising ability is incomplete. Consequently we must consider tests of a different nature to supplement those of knowledge described in the last chapter. The ideal situation is for both to complement and supplement each other: where confirmation of learned knowledge is required, a knowledge test can be performed, followed by a more practical test to confirm the learner's ability to put the knowledge into practice. In many cases, the knowledge test is an integral part of the practical test, ability to perform the task effectively implying possession of knowledge, without which performance of the task would not be possible. In many ways this is a preferable approach, with its less academic and more natural method of testing learning.

This chapter considers the design and construction of tests of a practical nature in the same way that knowledge/written tests were considered in the previous chapter, and covers tests of:

- skills – either operating, procedural or more general skills; usually practical, and which can be preceded by a written knowledge skill;
- attitudes and behaviour – usually practical, observational approaches.

These tests can be found at all stages of evaluation, but are more usually encountered as shown in Figure 5.1.

Their contributions to training, as with the written knowledge tests, are shown in Figure 5.2.

- PRIOR TO THE TRAINING AND DEVELOPMENT PROGRAMME
- AT THE START OF THE PROGRAMME
- PROGRESSIVELY DURING A PROGRAMME
- AT THE END OF THE EVENT

Figure 5.1 *Stages where skills, attitudes and behaviour tests are encountered*

- AN ASSESSMENT OF THE KNOWLEDGE, SKILLS AND ATTITUDES LEVELS PRIOR TO THE TRAINING
- THE MEASUREMENT OF LEARNING OVER THE PERIOD OF THE PROGRAMME
- SUPPORTING FEEDBACK TO LEARNERS DURING AN EVENT
- FEEDBACK TO THE TRAINERS OR OTHER PROGRAMME PRODUCERS ON THE EFFECTIVENESS OF THE TRAINING PROGRAMME

Figure 5.2 *Contributions of skills, attitudes and behaviour tests to training*

PRACTICAL DEMONSTRATION TESTS

These are probably the most straightforward of the practical skill tests and utilize the actual equipment or procedure to demonstrate the extent to which the learner is able to perform the skill etc. Obviously such a demonstration test is not necessary at the start of a programme if the training is to be concerned with a completely new type of machine etc, of which the learners have had no experience. To do this would be to embarrass the learners by demonstrating their inability. However, the test is relevant if the training is upgrading or remedial, the learners having had some prior knowledge or experience – in which case the extent of their (presumably limited) skill can be assessed.

Any method of using this approach is time-consuming, but what should be avoided is requiring a learner to demonstrate their skill (or lack of it) in front of a group. Demonstration should be individual, observation and assessment being made of each learner. Obviously this creates difficulties for a trainer in a group situation, but the *complete* demonstration need not be observed, or supporting observers and assessors can be drafted in for this purpose. The latter method is preferred so that the complete demonstration by the learner can be observed and any failings noted. If none of these alternatives is possible, learners can be paired to observe and assess each other, comprehensive advice being given for this assessment.

Figure 5.3 suggests a simple form for observation of a learner's practical demonstration; this can be replaced by a detailed checklist of all the aspects of operation to identify for future reference what the learner is capable or not capable of doing. If desirable, a scoring system can be incorporated rather than assessing a simple 'can do/can't do'.

VALIDATION OBSERVATION OF PRACTICAL DEMONSTRATION

1. Was the learner able to start the demonstration successfully? YES/NO
   (If 'no', no further answers are necessary.)
2. Did the learner complete the demonstration? YES/NO
   If 'yes', was it all completed correctly? YES/NO
   If 'yes' but all was not completed correctly, state
   which parts were incorrect:

   ....
   ....

3. Was the demonstration completed correctly for 10%, 25%,
   33%, 40%, 50%, 66%, 75%, 80%, 90%, 100%?
4. Could the learner explain where anything went wrong? YES/NO
   How?
5. How well were the objectives for the demonstration presented?
   Very clearly   6   5   4   3   2   1   Unclearly
6. How well was the object introduced at the start of the demonstration?
   Very well   6   5   4   3   2   1   Badly
7. How well was the purpose of the object or the end result of its
   operation described at the start?
   Very well   6   5   4   3   2   1   Badly
8. How clearly were the operating stages described?
   Very clearly   6   5   4   3   2   1   Unclearly
9. How clearly were the progressive operating steps demonstrated?
   Very clearly   6   5   4   3   2   1   Unclearly
10. How would you rate the learner's demonstration on the following scale?
    Excellent   8   7   6   5   4   3   2   1   0   Poor
11. Any other comments.

Figure 5.3 *Observation of practical demonstration*

Figure 5.4 suggests the format for a simple practical test in which the learner has to wire an electric plug.

ASSESSMENT OF LEARNER'S TEST IN ATTACHING A THREE-WIRE ELECTRIC CABLE TO A THREE-PIN PLUG

The learner was instructed to attach a three-wire electric cable to a three-pin plug, using the screwdriver and wire strippers provided. The finished item should satisfy all safety requirements.

1 Identifying the correct terminals for the relevant coloured wire. (If any of these are identified incorrectly, the result is an immediate fail.)
    Score 20 marks if this section is completed correctly.
2 Less than 2mm of bare wire is visible before the wire enters the terminal posts.
    Score 20 marks if correctly positioned.
    Deduct 6 points for each wire incorrectly positioned up to 5mm.
    Fail test if any wire's entry is greater than 5mm.
3 Each wire has been cut to correct length to enter terminal post correctly.
    Score 20 marks if all wires are cut correctly.
    Deduct 6 marks for each wire incorrectly cut up to 5mm.
    Deduct 20 marks if any wire length is in excess of 6mm.
4 The cable is held correctly, ie tightly but not overtightly, by the retention bar.
    Score 20 marks for correct location and tightening.
    Deduct 10 marks if the cable can move below the retention bar.
    Deduct 10 marks if the cable retention bar has been over-tightened.
5 The body retention screw has been tightened on closing the body.
    Score 20 marks for correct tightening.
    Deduct 15 marks if the screw is left slack.
    Immediate fail if the screw is not replaced.

Figure 5.4 *Practical task test*

DESIGN OF PRACTICAL DEMONSTRATION TESTS

Many of the guidelines identified in the construction of knowledge tests (see Figure 4.3) also relate to these tests, although the environment may be different.

- Ensure that the programme objectives are clear, logical and comprehensive
- Be careful of introducing short cuts
- Give full, open instructions of what is required
- Standardize the tests throughout the programme
- Tests must be as realistic as possible
- Consider breaking the tests into smaller training steps
- Give clear and complete instructions

---

1. Ensure that the objectives of the training programme are clear, logical and comprehensive. The test requirements will obviously be determined by these objectives, ie operate a particular piece of equipment, perform a particular activity on the computer, carry out a specific office procedure – all these should be defined in full, objective terms. One of the problems raised in training programmes of this nature concerning the completeness of the objectives is that determined by 'real life' practice. Experienced practitioners, through exposure to performing the task (perhaps within constraints) usually develop short cuts. Provided these short cuts are safe and do not detract in any way from the operation, they may of course be incorporated in the practice of the operation. But more frequently the short cuts do introduce some form of risk. Consequently the training *must* be for the complete and agreed practice – what happens at the workplace is the responsibility of the local manager of the operating staff.
2. The test should be introduced to the learners in as open a manner as possible, with full instructions and descriptions of what is required of them and how the assessment is to be made. What must be stressed, without appearing patronizing, is that the test is intended to help the learning and the training, and not as a means of demonstrating their failings.
3. The tests must be standardized so that all learners going through the same training programme perform the same test, under the

same conditions. This is fair, but it also validates the test and ensures that comparison between one learner or groups of learners can be made to validate the training process.

4. The test must be made as realistic as possible, replicating as far as possible the learners' working conditions. If a computer is to be used, it must be a similar model with equivalent software to that used by the learner at work.

5. In cases of complex operations it may be necessary to break the training down into smaller, logical steps: reflect this in the test, rather than expect the learner to be able to perform the whole in one activity. This can be helpful where parts of the process are not known by the learner at the start of the training.

6. Give clear and complete instructions, preferably orally *and* in writing, setting out what is required of the learner. These instructions, which again should be standardized, should include:

- the reasons for holding the test;
- the conditions under which the test will be held;
- any safety procedures that must be followed;
- the time available;
- that the demonstration will be observed and rated, the results of which will be fed back to the learners.

Other examples of this type of test are shown in Chapter 9, when the end of training validation is being considered.

TESTS OF PROCESS TASKS

Testing of operational tasks as described above is, in the main, a very objective, right/wrong approach. There are, however, many skills, particularly those at the management level, that are far from objective and must be approached in a different way. In fact some of these 'skills' are so subjective that some evaluation 'experts' say that for this very reason they cannot/should not be evaluated. If this argument is accepted, then the argument for any training is negated – if you cannot assess any change in the learners, particularly from a known starting point, how do you *know* that the training has been effective or worth doing? Of course, the assessment of subjective elements is difficult – impossible if total objectivity is demanded – but an approach to assessment can still be made. My criterion is that if the training is for objective tasks, the testing and assessment can be objective and objective tests must be used; if the tasks or processes are subjective, testing and assessment can only be by subjective means. In the latter case a consistent approach at least ensures some level of comparative assessment.

Some tasks and processes will obviously be more subjective than others. Some of the skills that fall into the least subjective categories are presentation, negotiation, interviewing and planning skills. The more subjective ones include skills of interpersonal relationships, people handling and assertiveness. However, in many ways the testing and assessment approaches are similar for both, the differences being a matter of objectivity scale. In some cases there are recognized and accepted models, whether the acceptance is general or restricted to the culture of the organization; in others the basis is an accepted 'good practice'; and in yet others an even less definable basis for acceptability.

ACTIVITY OBSERVATION OF PRACTICAL SKILLS

'Tests' at the start of training for the softer skills such as those of dealing with people – negotiation and the other processes mentioned above – are usually performed by observing the learners undertaking a relevant activity. The activity can be designed to include a number of aspects of the objectives for the training, and the observation is concerned with an assessment of to what extent the learners are aware of and use the methods, techniques and approaches of an effective process. For example, in negotiation training, the learners can be placed in pairs to negotiate with each other. Each negotiation is observed and assessed in line with the model of negotiation that has been agreed with the sponsor organization or a generally acceptable model. This observation will determine to a large extent the level of the learners, enabling a) a starting point to be established and b) confirmation of the extent of material needed to be included in the training event.

ACTIVITY OBSERVATION OF BEHAVIOURAL SKILLS

Testing and assessment of the highly subjective skills of interactive and interpersonal behaviour require exactly the same sort of observational assessment, the models on which the assessment is based being perhaps more subjective than those for, say, negotiation or presentation skills. But there must be some form of assessment at the start of the learning event, and this again will normally take the form of observation of the learners performing a relevant activity. In this case the activity will be one that allows the learners to interact, the extent and type of the interaction demonstrating the level of interactive and interpersonal skill held at that particular stage.

ACTIVITY OBSERVATION

The precise form of the observation will depend on the type of learning event, but can involve observation of the activity leader and also the group members (if the training is of a group nature), or of the principal individual in a one-to-one event such as interview training. Later in the programme observation may be devolved to the learners them- selves, but at the start of the programme the initial activity should be observed by the trainer who (it is assumed) is experienced in objective observation and assessment. For the same reasons, when 'testing' by activity takes place at the end of the programme, even though the learners may be observing their own activities completely by this stage, for assessment purposes the trainer must also be involved in the observational assessment. The final assessment can be a combi- nation of the observations of both the learners and the trainer.

Observation of the leader, members and interviewer

In group learning events in which activities are part of the programme it is usual for a group leader to be appointed, selected or elected from the group, this position rotating as the event progresses. The leader for the initial, early activity being assessed by the trainer should be appointed by the trainer, the appointee being, as far as possible, a member considered to be representative of the skills of the learning group. Of course, this is a highly subjective move, but it should give information on, for example, the leadership skills of that group of learners.

The trainer must be clear – based on the objectives for the event – what is necessary in the observation, and that this observation is as consistent as possible from one event to another. A standardized observation checklist is invaluable in this respect. There is a wide range available and to a large extent the one used will depend on the personal preferences of the observer, linked of course to the observation and programme objectives.

A general example of a leader observation assessment format is shown in Figure 5.5 and a more specific one in Figure 5.6.

LEADER OBSERVATION AND ASSESSMENT (1)

Observe the leader closely during the activity. Answer the questions posed and make short notes about any significant incidents relating to the leader's role fulfilment.

Did the leader:

TASK
Achieve the task? — How successfully?
Analyse and define the task? — How well?
Work to a plan? — Successfully?
Test ideas, proposals and solutions? — How often?
Make the best use of resources? — How?
Use all the information available or obtainable?

GROUP
Brief them effectively about the task?
Reach agreement on the objectives?
Agree the group process – timing, standards, procedures?
Summarize progress? — How often? How well?
Encourage the group to work together? — How?
Control the group? — How?
Keep the group on track?
Involve all the members in all parts of the process?

INDIVIDUAL
Ensure that each member had a role/task?
Check the understanding of each member about the task and their role? All? Only some? How?
Investigate special skills and knowledge?
Confirm the progress of each individual?
Ignore anybody?
Bring in each person as necessary?
Visibly upset anybody? Who? How?

Figure 5.5 *Leader observation and assessment format*

LEADER OBSERVATION AND ASSESSMENT (2)

1 How well did the leader introduce the task?
Very well   6   5   4   3   2   1   Badly

2 To what extent did the leader ensure that the task was understood?
Very well   6   5   4   3   2   1   Badly

3 How well did the leader organize the group for the task?
Very well   6   5   4   3   2   1   Badly

4 How well did the leader seek the views of the group in problem identification?
Very well   6   5   4   3   2   1   Badly

5 How well did the leader seek the views of the group in problem solution?
Very well   6   5   4   3   2   1   Badly

6 How well did the leader encourage the members to interact effectively?
Very well   6   5   4   3   2   1   Badly

7 How effective was the leader's style?
Very good   6   5   4   3   2   1   Poor

8 To what extent did the leader contribute, rather than the members?
A lot   6   5   4   3   2   1   Little

9 How well did the leader bring in the quieter members?
Very well   6   5   4   3   2   1   Badly

10 How well did the leader ensure everybody was heard?
Very well   6   5   4   3   2   1   Badly

11 To what extent did the leader seek alternative proposals/ solutions etc?
A lot   6   5   4   3   2   1   Little

12 To what extent did the leader seek alternative decisions?
A lot   6   5   4   3   2   1   Little

13 How effective were the leadership techniques used?
Very good   6   5   4   3   2   1   Poor

14 How effective overall were the leader's communication skills?
Very good   6   5   4   3   2   1   Poor

Figure 5.6 *Leader observation and assessment format (rated)*

A similar format for observing the members of the group is shown as Figure 5.7.

MEMBER OBSERVATION AND ASSESSMENT

1 How well did the members show that they understood the task?
   Very well   6   5   4   3   2   1   Badly

2 To what extent did the members identify the problem?
   Fully   6   5   4   3   2   1   Not at all

3 To what extent did the members involve themselves in the discussions?
   Fully   6   5   4   3   2   1   Not at all

4 To what extent did the group offer alternative solutions?
   Fully   6   5   4   3   2   1   Not at all

5 How wide a range of possible solutions did the members give?
   Very wide   6   5   4   3   2   1   Not at all wide

6 To what extent did the group involve themselves in the decision making?
   Fully   6   5   4   3   2   1   Not at all

7 To what extent did the members contribute overall?
   Fully   6   5   4   3   2   1   Not at all

8 To what extent did the members stick to the task?
   Fully   6   5   4   3   2   1   Not at all

9 How much notice was taken of the leader's views?
   A lot   6   5   4   3   2   1   Not at all

10 How much did the members interrupt each other?
   A lot   6   5   4   3   2   1   Not at all

11 How much did the members appear to listen to each other?
   A lot   6   5   4   3   2   1   Not at all

12 Overall, how effective were the members in this task?
   Very good   6   5   4   3   2   1   Poor

Any comments about individual members?

Figure 5.7   *Member observation and assessment format (rated)*

An example format for observing the interviewer in a one-to-one interaction is shown in Figure 5.8.

INTERVIEWER OBSERVATION AND ASSESSMENT

1   How well did the interviewer open the interview?
    Very well   6   5   4   3   2   1   Badly
2   How well did the interviewer follow an effective structure?
    Very well   6   5   4   3   2   1   Badly
3   To what extent did the interviewer explain this structure to the interviewee?
    Completely 6   5   4   3   2   1   Not at all
4   How well did the interviewer terminate the interview?
    Very well   6   5   4   3   2   1   Badly
5   To what extent was the interviewer aware of the interviewee's reactions?
    Completely 6   5   4   3   2   1   Not at all
6   How quickly was rapport achieved?
    Quickly   6   5   4   3   2   1   Not at all
7   To what extent was the interviewee encouraged to talk?
    Completely 6   5   4   3   2   1   Not at all
8   How well did the interviewer construct and pose his/her questions?
    Very well   6   5   4   3   2   1   Badly
9   How prescriptive was the interviewer?
    Very   6   5   4   3   2   1   Not at all
10 To what extent did the interviewer appear to be listening?
    Completely 6   5   4   3   2   1   Not at all
11 To what extent did the interviewer appear to be interested?
    Completely 6   5   4   3   2   1   Not at all
12 To what extent did the interviewer interrupt the interviewee?
    A lot   6   5   4   3   2   1   Not at all
13 To what extent did the interview achieve the interviewer's objectives?
    Completely 6   5   4   3   2   1   Not at all
14 To what extent did the interview achieve the interviewee's objectives?
    Completely 6   5   4   3   2   1   Not at all

Figure 5.8 *Interviewer observation and assessment format (rated)*

These are simply *examples* of formats. They can be varied considerably as needed, although the basis will probably be the same in all cases, namely an assessment of the skill at that point in time of the people being observed. They can be used at the start of the event, as a final assessment and, with more open questions, as general observation instruments by the learners themselves during the event when activities take place. The extent of the observation of individuals will obviously depend on the number of observers available – normally one trainer cannot observe everybody him- or herself; again a cohort of supporting observers can be introduced.

It is accepted that the leader observation is for one member only, where one activity only is taking place and one trainer only is available, but other arrangements are possible and other members can be given a rough, initial assessment as they take on the leader's role. Assessment of the members must, of necessity, be general and not concentrate on individuals. Again, this is less than desirable, but it at least it gives some information. It is possible, however, using other types of instruments to chart the progress of individual members from the start of an event through to the end.

More general observation instruments and formats can be useful to both the trainer and the participants when the interview is being debriefed – perhaps even more so when the participants alone are conducting the debrief. Figure 5.9 gives an example of a debrief reflection and debrief *aide mémoire*.

OBSERVATION OF BEHAVIOUR

You will see that, in the types of learning events we are discussing here, observation as suggested above not only considers the task application and the processes used, but also any specific and significant behaviours involved. However, there are occasions when behaviour specifically needs to be observed and assessed. Observations of this nature are generally referred to as activity analyses, and more particularly behaviour analysis. This is such an important form of observation assessment, which can also be linked with task observation, that Chapter 6 is devoted to it. Particular emphasis will be placed on a specific form of behaviour observation, Behaviour Analysis.

FOR THE INTERVIEWER

1. How well do you feel that you coped with the situation presented to you?
2. Why do you feel that?
3. What type of structure did you try to apply to the interview?
4. How successful do you think you were in this?
5. What problems or problem areas occurred during the interview?
6. How (well) did you deal with these?
7. To what extent do you feel your behaviour affected the interview?
8. Could you have behaved in any other (more effective) manner?
9. To what extent did you help the interviewee? How?
10. To what extent did you hinder the interviewee? How?
11. How did you feel about the behaviour and actions of the interviewee in
    - helping you with the interview?
    - hindering you?

FOR THE INTERVIEWEE

1. How did you feel about your role in the interview?
2. How realistic did you feel the activity was?
3. What problems were caused for you?
4. How did these problems arise?
5. How were the problems handled and who handled them – you or the interviewer?
6. To what extent did the interviewer:
7. – help you?
8. – hinder you?
9. How well (sympathetically) were you received in the interview?
10. Who produced the possible solutions to the problem(s)?
11. Who suggested the final action to be taken?
12. Would you have wanted this any other way?
13. Did you readily accept the suggested action?
14. If you had been the interviewer, what would you have done differently?

Figure 5.9 *One-to-one activity reflection and debrief aide mémoire*

6

Behaviour Observation and Self-reporting

Several methods of observing the practical activities of learners were considered in Chapter 5, the emphasis being on the observation for assessment purposes of their performance of the task. Without a band of observers, it is obvious that individual members cannot be assessed in this way, with the exception perhaps of the leader of the group. But even in this case, the observation will be of one individual only at that particular time. In order to assess individuals performing a task, it is necessary to use a different form of assessment observation – activity and behaviour analysis. In the majority of cases this observation will be of processes employed by learner participants rather than the adherence to a task model. However, this type of observation can lend itself to modification for task observation, eg observation of an interviewer in a one-to-one situation as described in the previous chapter, or of two participants in a negotiation activity (this will be demonstrated later in this chapter).

ACTIVITY ANALYSIS

If we need to observe a group of people to assess the level of their activity at a particular point in time, the simplest approach is known as *simple contribution scoring*. This, as its name implies is a) simple and b) scores, or counts, the number of contributions made by the individuals over a particular period of time. A *contribution* in verbal activity analysis is defined as the occasion when a person speaks or does something that is allied to speaking, eg interrupts someone while they are speaking. Contributions can also be non-verbal – gestures, movements, facial expressions and so on – and these are usually the subject of an activity analysis separate to the verbal analysis, simply because it is very difficult to observe and record both verbal and non-verbal contributions at the same time.

THE SIMPLE CONTRIBUTION SCORING APPROACH

The simple contribution scoring approach takes the form of the trainer or other observer sitting outside the participating group and making a note of the number of times each member makes a contribution. Usually the annotation takes the form of a vertical stroke for each contribution, to build up five-barred gates that can be counted easily. Figure 6.1 shows part of a completed scoring sheet for a group of six participants.

Mary	‖‖‖ ‖‖‖ ‖‖‖ ‖‖‖ ‖‖‖ ‖‖‖ ‖‖‖ |||	18
John	‖‖‖ ‖‖‖ ||	12
Celia	||	2
Frank	‖‖‖ ‖‖‖ ‖‖‖ ‖‖‖ ‖‖‖ ||	27
Edna	‖‖‖ ‖‖‖ ‖‖‖ ‖‖‖	20
Bill	‖‖‖	5
Total contributions		84

Figure 6.1 *Simple contribution scoring*

The scoring shown in Figure 6.1 produces information about the total number of contributions made in the group as a whole – this, when compared with other groups, assesses the activity level of the group in terms of verbal contributions. It also shows the number of contributions made by each member of the group – ie the number of times each person spoke, thus demonstrating the comparative contribution activity of each. It will be seen immediately that Frank was the most verbally active member, with Edna coming second, followed closely by Mary. On the other hand, Celia only spoke twice, and Bill five times. If the artificial average is calculated (14), John is closest to being the average contributor in this particular group.

Of course, the scoring does not tell us how long each person spoke, the value of their contribution, the order of their speaking etc. For example, even though Celia only spoke twice, those contributions may have been the most valuable in the whole discussion – but if so, why did she (was she allowed to) speak only twice? Could it be that she was unable to get a word in because of Frank? Other observation will give this type of information, but the simple scoring is highly objective in its quantity approach.

It is sometimes valuable to identify the order in which people speak – for example, Celia's contributions may have been early in the discussion, and either started the discussion along the right lines or were ignored, so that she did not bother to speak again. Instead of simple strokes, a progressive numerical sequence can be used – 1, 2, 3, 4 etc. So, if Celia was the first to speak, her first 'stroke' would be 1; then Frank spoke – 2 – and so on. The weight of the contribution can be indicated by the length of time the individual speaks – a stroke might be entered every ten seconds (a period that with a little practice can be estimated) of the contribution. For example, if Frank was not only a high contributor, but a long-winded one too, the number of strokes against his name might now total 125.

Obviously this analysis method is limited, but there are occasions when only simple information is required.

THE DIRECTIONAL SOCIOGRAM

At a slightly more complex level than simple scoring is the directional sociogram, which as its name implies is concerned with the direction of discussion. The scoring in this approach can be linked with simple contribution scoring, and other more sophisticated activities can also be included.

The observer starts with a sheet of paper on which circles are placed, representing the members of the group. Lines are drawn between each circle to represent the line of communication between the members, and from each circle another line is drawn outwards from the centre. Figure 6.2 shows this starting point.

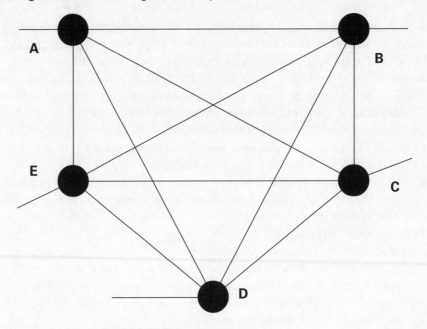

Figure 6.2 *Initial directional sociogram*

Figure 6.3 is an example of a completed sociogram.

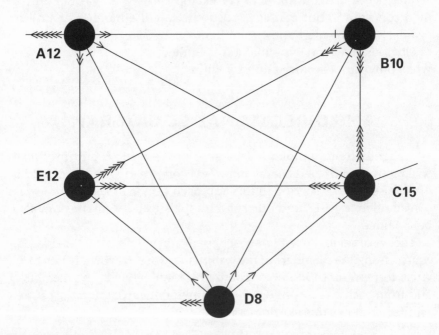

Figure 6.3 *Completed directional sociogram*

As each participant makes a contribution an arrow is added to the line joining them to the participant to whom the contribution has been made. If the contribution is made to the group in general the arrows are placed on the lines pointing out from the group. A further 'score' can be noted by placing a stroke across the line when an interruption is made. The figure beside a member's letter shows the number of contributions made by that person during the period of observation.

Figure 6.3 shows that the particular activity observed – part of a discussion – in fact divided into sub-groups. Member D was almost completely isolated, being interrupted by everybody, with members B and C the only members to whom D was able to speak – but with little success! Finally D was reduced to making contributions to the group as a whole, but nobody replied. B, C and E formed a sub-group of three, in the main speaking only to each other. The leader, A, was ignored by E, interrupted by B and C and, like D, was forced to make most contributions to the group as a whole – again mainly being ignored.

Again, directional sociograms do not give the complete story of the group activity, but they do give rather more than the simple record and can be very useful when applied when this type of information is required.

BEHAVIOUR ANALYSIS

This approach to behavioural observation and assessment concentrates on the interpersonal behaviour exhibited by the learners in a variety of situations. It is based on the use of a selection of categories of behaviour, most of which occur in most situations, although there are one or two that have specific reference or *should* occur in an effective interaction. The incidence of these behaviours is observed and recorded and enables subsequent analysis of the behaviour of the people observed.

Before behaviour analysis can be attempted, the observer must be aware of the categories to be observed – what they are and how they can be identified. A crucial word in this approach is 'identification' – in behaviour analysis the observation of individuals is concerned with identifying, not interpreting, the behaviours exhibited. In the majority of cases reactions are to observed behaviour rather than what the person exhibiting the behaviour *meant* to express. Observations can be as specific as required, concentrating on behaviours that should take place in a task or role, or can be more general, considering overall human behaviour.

BEHAVIOUR CATEGORY DESCRIPTIONS

The behaviours observed in behaviour analysis are called categories and have specific definitions which help in the identification of an observation. These have been investigated to a considerable extent by such researchers as Neil Rackham and Terry Morgan (1977), Neil Rackham and others (1971) and Peter Honey (1988), among others, and they have developed an analysis instrument that is known as Behaviour Analysis.

The categories described by these researchers can be for general use, in one-to-one interactions, in meetings and so on.

Interview analysis

The range of frequent behaviours is well known and consists of:

Seeking information, in which one individual asks questions of another.
Giving information, views, feelings, opinions, usually in response to a question.
Seeking ideas, in which someone (usually the interviewer) asks the other for positive ideas or proposals.
Proposals, in which an individual proposes, suggests or otherwise puts forward their views on how action might be taken. These can be expressed as:

> 'I propose that . . .'
> 'I suggest that we . . .'
> 'Let's do . . .'
> 'I think your approach should be . . .'
> 'What do you think about the idea that we . . .?'.

Building, which takes the form of another proposal, but instead of giving a contrasting alternative, supports the original proposal by adding further ideas that add value to the original.
Supporting, in which a positive expression of support for another's views or proposals is made.
Disagreeing in this analysis is the blunt, often aggressive form of disagreeing with the speaker.
Disagreeing (with reasons): here the disagreement is not a blunt statement, but is supported by the disagreer's reasons.
Testing understanding is again usually a behaviour exhibited by the interviewer to check out whether they have understood what the

interviewee has said, or whether the interviewee has understood the interviewer.

Summarizing is a behaviour exhibited, although not exclusively, by the interviewer, in which what has been discussed, proposed or agreed is repeated in summary form for agreement.

Open behaviour is exhibited by the speaker accepting verbally that they were wrong or apologizing for some incident, in a contribution sometimes as simple as 'I'm sorry'.

Attacking/Blocking. These two categories are usually linked together as they both express negative rather than positive behaviour. 'Attacking' is when the statement made by the speaker is openly aggressive or abusive and has an emotional content. An example of this might be 'I might have expected *you* to say that!' which the receiver would see as an attack on their contribution and themselves. This usually produces a defensive response, frequently in the form of a counter-attack – and so on.

'Blocking' is a behavioural contribution that adds little or nothing positive to an interaction and in fact can often stop it altogether. The bland and unsupported statement 'Oh, we're just getting nowhere' is a common example which, if stated as bluntly as this, simply stops the discussion, and positive action has to be taken by somebody to move the interaction on.

Interrupting. This can take several forms with the individual making a contribution before the speaker has finished speaking, effectively saying 'Shut up. I have something much more important to say!' Or an individual can respond to a question when the question was posed to somebody else – the interrupter is again saying 'My answer is much more important than yours!' If two people carry on a side conversation while others are taking part in a discussion they are interrupting the others by a) not listening to what they are saying – 'Our thoughts are more important than yours' and b) implying they do not share their views, which of course may be important.

Bringing in occurs when a question is posed or an invitation to contribute is given to a specific person, usually by naming them.

Other behaviour categories are usually sub-divisions of these or perhaps less frequent types of behaviour. Some behaviours occur in certain situations more than in others and are often more significant. In such cases, the behaviour analysis usually concentrates on these. Let us take the case of an appraisal interview between a boss and a member of their staff. The significant behaviours in this case would include most of the list above, but could be more specifically defined as:

- seeking ideas;
- proposing;
- building;
- seeking information by asking questions;
- open, closed, leading and multiple questions;
- reflecting – restatements of what the speaker has just said, usually made with the intention of encouraging the speaker to continue with that topic, eg 'You seem to feel that it is time you did something about . . .', expressed as a statement, not as a question;
- giving information, views, feelings etc;
- disagreeing (both types);
- testing understanding;
- summarizing;
- open behaviour;
- attacking/blocking;
- interrupting;
- bringing in.

This list of categories may seem long and difficult to use, but there are only two people involved in the interaction and, in the main, only one is speaking at once. Consequently the behaviours occur at a slower pace than in the case of a group activity.

A behaviour analysis observation is performed by the observer annotating a sheet with contribution strokes, as in simple contribution scoring. But instead of strokes being made simply for each contribution, the speaker is identified and also the category of behaviour, the stroke being entered against these, in the column relating to the speaker at the row relating to the category. In this way the number of contributions and their types can be identified in an analysis at the end of the interaction and compared with a model of an effective interaction. A sample form for observing a one-to-one interaction is included here as Figure 6.4.

Group behaviour analysis

Analysis of the behaviour observable in a group is more difficult than in the one-to-one situation purely because the activity is usually greater and faster, and there are more people to observe and record. However, a relatively experienced observer should find little difficulty in analysing a group of six to eight people, using a behaviour analysis sheet with 11 to 13 categories. The greater the number of categories, the more difficult the observation, but the more accurate the analysis. The increase in numbers above six, or even above eight, does not

BEHAVIOUR ANALYSIS: ONE-TO-ONE ACTIVITY.............. Period of observation..............................	INTERVIEWER	INTERVIEWEE
Proposing		
Building		
Seeking ideas		
Asking open questions		
Asking closed questions		
Asking leading questions		
Asking multiple questions		
Asking other questions		
Giving information		
Testing understanding		
Summarizing		
Open behaviour		
Attacking/blocking		
Interrupting		
Bringing in		
Totals		

Figure 6.4   *A one-to-one observation BA sheet*

necessarily increase the difficulties because, after all, most of the time only one person will be speaking at a time. The major difficulty occurs when the activity increases frantically and contributions happen in rapid succession, or even overlap. Figure 6.5 demonstrates an example of a completed behaviour analysis observation sheet for a group.

SELECTING CATEGORIES

Naturally behaviour analysis observation instruments can be designed for a wide range of activities, analysing from a limited number of

BEHAVIOUR ANALYSIS: ACTIVITY............................ Period of observation....................................							
	John	Mike	Sally	Jean	Ralph	Mary	Totals
Proposing	9	15		1	15	4	44
Building	1			1		1	3
Seeking ideas	5			1	1		7
Seeking information	16	6	1	5	15	19	62
Giving information	12	22	12	14	14	25	99
Testing understanding		8			1		9
Summarizing	7		12		1		20
Open behaviour	3					6	9
Attacking/blocking		8	1	4	12	8	33
Interrupting	6	15	1	6	8	14	50
Bringing in		15	3	2			20
Totals	59	89	30	34	67	77	356

Figure 6.5 *A group 11-category BA sheet*

categories to as many as the observer can manage, and different categories related to the type of activity. Non-verbal behaviour can be observed, although experience suggests that these observations have less value than those for verbal behaviour, as non-verbal signals are prone to misidentification and therefore misinterpretation. However, a list of non-verbal categories can be developed in the same way as for their verbal relations.

The list of categories does not have to be as extensive as suggested, which will make the observation simpler, but it must be remembered that the less detailed the analysis, the less specific information becomes available, with consequently a possible reduction in effectiveness. An example of a simple analysis instrument is given in Figure 6.6, although it does require some element of interpretation rather than straight-forward identification of behaviour – and interpretation of somebody else's behaviour can easily be wrong!

BEHAVIOUR CATEGORIES	FREQUENCY OF OCCURRENCES/ PARTICIPANTS						
PROPOSING							
QUESTIONING							
GIVING INFORMATION ETC							
OTHER POSITIVE CONTRIBUTIONS							
OTHER NEGATIVE CONTRIBUTIONS							
TOTALS							

Figure 6.6 *Simple behaviour analysis instrument*

CRITERIA FOR SELECTING CATEGORIES

Unless you are going to use the full-category type of analysis sheet, you will be making decisions about which categories you want to include for a particular type of event. Some guidelines are described here:

1. Determine the basic categories to be observed according to the objectives for the event and the type of event. For example, some of the categories that would be used in a behaviour analysis sheet for a negotiation would be different from those for a problem-solving activity.
2. Within the range of objectives, particularly if the results are to be fed back to the learners to facilitate learning and change, only include categories that are capable of change. There is little purpose in observing a behaviour if, with whatever training, it is such an inherent personal foible that training could not change it.
3. Select behaviours, verbally or non-verbally, that can be observed. For example, a verbal proposal will be reasonably readily identified, as will a non-verbal signal such as a smile. Any 'behaviour' that requires interpretation should be excluded, as one person's interpretation is another's different interpretation.
4. Be honest about the behaviour – not one that you are expecting, hoping for or anticipating intuitively.
5. Focus on the significant behaviours – it may be satisfying to be able to analyse a large number of behaviours, but it is a waste of time if many of them have no significance.

6. Each category must be significantly different from any other. If they are not, there will be an inclination to (mis)interpret to which category a contribution belongs.

7. The category description must be clear and in as simple language as possible so that the observer has no difficulty in identifying the category into which a behaviour should go. Trained observers may, however, modify this requirement if the results are to be used by themselves only and they are accustomed to a different language or jargon.

8. The categories must demonstrate high inter-observer reliability so that they can be used consistently by several observers.

9. Organize the categories on the observation sheet into the rough logical order in which the actual behaviours will occur. However, do not rely on this sequence of behaviour, or the system will fall down as the activity progresses.

Whichever form of behaviour analysis is selected, it can be used throughout the training programme. The intention of raising the subject at this stage is that it be used by the trainer at the start of the event, but behaviour analyses can be used throughout the programme, by both the trainer and the learners (with some training in its use), and again at the end of the event to identify any changes that might have occurred. When a number of analysis observations have been performed, particularly in an interpersonal skills programme, the analyses can be summarized for feedback to the learners at a relevant stage during the event and also at the end. An example of this feedback matrix will be given in Chapter 7, Figure 7.1.

SELF-REPORTING TESTS

There will be occasions when direct observation for the purposes of assessment will not be possible or desirable and some form of assessment has to be achieved by other means. One approach is to use the learners to report on themselves: obviously such reporting may be very subjective, biased, perhaps distorted, and highly susceptible to both wishful thinking and to misreporting – either deliberately or because of an erroneous belief on the part of the learner. But if this is the only means of assessment possible, it should be used, bearing these caveats in mind.

The basic approach is to have the learners complete a questionnaire that asks how they see themselves in certain situations, or the extent of their knowledge, skills or attitudes. The same questionnaire must be completed at the start of the training and at the end. However, I believe that this simplistic approach creates many problems and inconsistencies, and I describe in Chapter 8 what I call the three-test, which in most cases provides a more realistic form of before and after comparison.

A self-reporting questionnaire usually poses questions about the learners' impressions of themselves and seeks their views, self-assessed on a scoring scale. For example, questions about a learner's communication skills might include the following.

Please ring the score that you feel represents you at this stage. Enter how you think it really is, not what it should be or what somebody would want it to be.

I   How do you feel you communicate with your senior managers?
    Very well 10 9 8 7 6 5 4 3 2 1 Badly
2   How well do you feel you communicate with your peers?
    Very well 10 9 8 7 6 5 4 3 2 1 Badly
3   How well do you feel you communicate with your subordinates?
    Very well 10 9 8 7 6 5 4 3 2 1 Badly
4   How well do you feel you communicate in writing?
    Very well 10 9 8 7 6 5 4 3 2 1 Badly
5   How well do you feel you communicate verbally?
    Very well 10 9 8 7 6 5 4 3 2 1 Badly
and so on.

The results of this questionnaire should then be collected and can be entered on a spreadsheet for later comparison at the end of the programme (a fuller description of the process will be given in Chapter 8 when the end of programme validation is being considered). Figure 6.7 gives an example that I have frequently used in connection with an interpersonal skills training programme.

REFLECTIVE SELF-REPORTING

The most successful self-reporting approach is when a questionnaire is completed at the end of an activity and linked with consideration of the actions of others and how they might have affected the individual. The process for this, immediately after the activity – exercise, discussion, interview etc – is to ask the participants to reflect on what

Please ring each item in the scores 10 to 1 representing where your present level of skill might be.

HIGH   LOW

1   Being aware of my own behaviour
            10   9   8   7   6   5   4   3   2   1
2   Being aware of the behaviour of others
            10   9   8   7   6   5   4   3   2   1
3   Being aware of the reactions of others to my behaviour
            10   9   8   7   6   5   4   3   2   1
4   Being aware of my reaction to the behaviour of others
            10   9   8   7   6   5   4   3   2   1
5   Being aware of how much I talk
            10   9   8   7   6   5   4   3   2   1
6   Being aware of how much I support others
            10   9   8   7   6   5   4   3   2   1
7   Being aware of how much I build on the ideas of others
            10   9   8   7   6   5   4   3   2   1
8   Sensing the feelings of others
            10   9   8   7   6   5   4   3   2   1
9   Being aware of how much I interrupt others
            10   9   8   7   6   5   4   3   2   1
10 Being aware of how much I really listen to others
            10   9   8   7   6   5   4   3   2   1
11 Telling others what my feelings are
            10   9   8   7   6   5   4   3   2   1
12 Being aware of what behaviour modification I need to do
            10   9   8   7   6   5   4   3   2   1
13 Knowing how to modify my behaviour
            10   9   8   7   6   5   4   3   2   1
14 Being aware of how much I bring out the views of others
            10   9   8   7   6   5   4   3   2   1

Figure 6.7   *Interpersonal skills self-reporting questionnaire*

happened during the activity, who was responsible, what resulted and so on. This can be achieved simply by individual reflection followed by a discussion based on participants' thoughts. But the activity will be more effective if they are given something concrete to help them marshal their thoughts – a self-questionnaire. Figure 6.8 suggests a questionnaire for the activity leader's reflection and Figure 6.9 one for the group members.

ACTIVITY SELF-ANALYSIS (LEADER)

Where relevant, please allocate a score to each of the items, as you saw them, by circling the number you feel best applies to that particular aspect. Add some brief notes to remind yourself of the reason why you have given this score and otherwise add some brief notes. You will be able to refer to this questionnaire in the activity review that follows.

	Good, very or a lot			Poor, not very or not very much		

THE ACTIVITY AND THE TASK

How successful do you feel you were in achieving the task?	6	5	4	3	2	1
How difficult did you find the task?	6	5	4	3	2	1
How good was the time allocation for the activity?	6	5	4	3	2	1
To what extent did you work to a plan?	6	5	4	3	2	1
Was this plan agreed by all the members?	6	5	4	3	2	1
To what extent did you make use of all the resources at your disposal?	6	5	4	3	2	1
To what extent did you make use of all the information available or obtainable?	6	5	4	3	2	1
What were the major factors involved in the success or failure?						

YOURSELF

How effective do you feel your leadership was?	6	5	4	3	2	1
To what extent did you ensure the members knew what they had to do?	6	5	4	3	2	1
To what extent did you confirm the progress of each member during the activity?	6	5	4	3	2	1
To what extent did you bring everybody in?	6	5	4	3	2	1
How much did you ignore any member?	6	5	4	3	2	1
How often did you summarize progress?	6	5	4	3	2	1
Did you have many problems as a leader?	6	5	4	3	2	1
What were they and how did you overcome them?						
What did you do that helped the process most?						
What did you do that hindered the process most?						
Was there anything else you could have done to have helped the activity and the members?						
If you had been a member instead of leader, what would you have done?						
If you had to repeat the activity, what changes would you make?						
How would you rate yourself as the leader in that activity?	6	5	4	3	2	1

THE MEMBERS

How helpful were your group members in the achievement of the activity?	6	5	4	3	2	1
How hindering were your group members in processing the activity?	6	5	4	3	2	1
How did these helps or hindrances show themselves?						
What else would you have liked your members to have done?						
How do you think your members will score you as the leader?	6	5	4	3	2	1
What have you learned from the activity that you might be able to implement on your return to work?						

Figure 6.8 *Activity questionnaire (leader)*

ACTIVITY SELF-ANALYSIS (GROUP MEMBER)

Where relevant, please allocate a score to each of the items, as you saw them, by circling the number you feel best applies to that particular aspect. Add some brief notes to remind yourself of the reason why you have given this score and otherwise add some brief notes. You will be able to refer to this questionnaire in the activity review that follows.

	Good, very or a lot			Poor, not very or not very much		

THE ACTIVITY AND THE TASK

How successful do you feel you were in achieving the task?	6	5	4	3	2	1
How difficult did you find the task?	6	5	4	3	2	1
How good was the time allocation for the activity?	6	5	4	3	2	1
To what extent did you work to a plan?	6	5	4	3	2	1
Was this plan agreed by all the members?	6	5	4	3	2	1
To what extent did the leader make use of all the resources at your disposal?	6	5	4	3	2	1
To what extent did the leader make use of all the information available or obtainable?	6	5	4	3	2	1
What were the major factors involved in the success or failure?						

YOURSELF

How effective do you feel your participation was?	6	5	4	3	2	1
To what extent did you know what you had to do?	6	5	4	3	2	1
Did you have many problems as a member?	6	5	4	3	2	1

What were they and how did you overcome them?
What did you do that helped the process most?
What did you do that hindered the process most?
Was there anything else you could have done to have helped the activity, the other members and the leader?
If you had been leader instead of a member, what would you have done?
If you had to repeat the activity, what changes would you make?

THE LEADER

To what extent did the leader confirm the progress of each member during the activity?	6	5	4	3	2	1
To what extent did the leader bring everybody in?	6	5	4	3	2	1
How much did the leader ignore any member?	6	5	4	3	2	1
How often did the leader summarize progress?	6	5	4	3	2	1
How helpful was the leader to the members in the achievement of the activity?	6	5	4	3	2	1
How hindering was the leader in processing the activity?	6	5	4	3	2	1
How did these helps or hindrances show themselves?						
What else would you have liked your leader to have done?						
How would you rate the leader in that activity?	6	5	4	3	2	1
What have you learned from the activity that you might be able to implement on your return to work?						

Figure 6.9 *Activity questionnaire (group member)*

SELECTING THE APPROPRIATE TECHNIQUE

Some of the commonest testing techniques that are available for use at the start of a training and development programme have been described in this and the previous chapter. It is necessary to bear in mind that if a test is used at this stage it will almost certainly be used again at the end of the programme. Figure 6.10 summarizes the most appropriate testing techniques for various types of training and development programmes.

Types of training	Testing techniques
Knowledge of facts etc	Written test
Practical skills and procedures	Practical demonstration
General skills	Activity analysis Behaviour analysis
Interpersonal skills	Behaviour analysis

Figure 6.10 *Summary of training and testing techniques*

7

—

Interim Evaluation

An effective trainer will be evaluating the effectiveness of the learning programme as it progresses, usually in an informal manner – observing the activities of the learners, assessing their understanding by questioning and so on. Of course, these observations are subjective, but none the less valuable for this. There are, however, more formal and objective approaches that can, and should be used during a programme, particularly one lasting more than a day. The more frequently used of these will include:

- ACTIVITY ANALYSIS
- BEHAVIOUR ANALYSIS
- PRACTICAL TESTS AND DEMONSTRATIONS
- DIURNAL REVIEWS OR AUDITS
- SPOT CHECKS
- SESSION REVIEWS
- LOGBOOK REVIEWS

INTERIM EVALUATION CAVEAT

Before progressing further, you must be aware of a major danger in introducing interim evaluation measures, particularly when the learners are aware of the evaluation and are contributing to it directly. The purpose of the interim evaluation is to assess how well the training is achieving its objectives and the learners are learning.

If the evaluation shows that all is not progressing as it should, you must do something about it.

This involves the use of time, and you must be certain that your programme resources will allow this.

If you are unable to take the necessary action, there is little point in performing the evaluation.

ACTIVITY ANALYSIS

This approach was described in Chapters 5 and 6 as a means of assessing the starting position of the learners. The actual forms included the use of assessment questionnaires, simple contribution scoring, directional sociograms etc. All these can be continued during the programme whenever activities take place. Usually they are not performed primarily for evaluation purposes, rather for immediate information feedback to the learners, but if they are written analyses they can be retained and referred to as progressive evaluation measures. However, the more common practice nowadays is to use the learners themselves to observe and feed back their observations to the remainder of the learning group. Consequently fully consistent and valid material may not be available to the trainer for evaluation, but of course (unless they have other tasks to perform) the trainers can perform parallel observations for their own evaluation.

BEHAVIOUR ANALYSIS

The same comments apply to behaviour analysis that were made above for activity analysis, except that normally the analysis observation is performed by the trainers rather than the learners. However, in spite of some difficulties, the learners on certain programmes can be taught (perhaps in a limited form) behaviour analysis approaches such as those described in Chapter 6.

In an interpersonal skills programme, the trainers will usually be maintaining a continuous series of behaviour analysis observations of all the activities in which the learners are participating. The principal reason for these observations is to give feedback to the learners on how they have behaved during the programme to a particular point. But the learners' progress and the validity of the learning programme are also being evaluated. As the programme progresses a number of learning aspects should and do evolve, and part of the design of the programme is to enable this to happen. If it is not happening as intended, this is good feedback evaluation for the trainer, evaluation that points to programme modifications that can be introduced there and then.

ANALYSIS SUMMARY

The principal objectives of an interpersonal or similar skills programme are to a) help the learners to become aware of their behaviour and skills and b) provide the opportunity for the learners to start to modify behaviour with which they are then not satisfied. The progressive and continuous observation should help in this process, giving the learners factual information about these behaviours, followed by activities designed to enable the modifications to be attempted. Again this reporting, and the success of the modifications, are part of a total programme evaluation process.

If behaviour analysis observations are carried out using an observation instrument such as that shown in Figure 6.5, at a particular point in the programme the observations can be summarized and presented to the learners as feedback of their behaviour to that stage. An example of this is shown as Figure 7.1.

Here the horizontal rows represent the behavioural categories over which the individual has been observed for the activities involved. The vertical columns give a wealth of information, recording the number of contributions made by the individual (the figure in the left of the box), and (in the right of the box) that raw figure expressed as a percentage of their total contributions in that activity. At the foot of the columns for each activity, the figures show a) the total of their personal contributions compared with the total contributions of the group and b) that equation compared with the group average in that activity.

The final column averages out their behaviours in the same way. Thus the individual can see to what extent they contributed during each activity and what they said (the category), how they compared with the rest of the group in that activity, and a profile of their behaviour compared with that of the group over the total of events observed and recorded.

ONE-TO-ONE INTERACTION ANALYSIS

If the programme has been concerned with the skills and behavioural skills of one-to-one interviewing or similar interactions, the same sort of behaviour analyses may have been performed and an interim

Category / Activity	A	B	C	D	E	F	Average
PROPOSING	2 2%	6 11%		3 16%	1 3%		2 5%
SUGGESTING		1 2%					– –
BUILDING	1 2%						– –
SEEKING IDEAS	1 11%	1 2%					– –
SEEKING INFORMATION	14 14%	9 17%	3 10%	1 3%	4 21%	1 3%	5 11%
TESTING UNDERSTANDING	2 2%	1 2%					1 2%
GIVING INFORMATION	43 43%	23 43%	19 63%	24 77%	7 37%	16 43%	22 50%
DISAGREEING + REASONS	11 11%					1 3%	2 5%
SUMMARIZING							– –
SUPPORTING	5 5%	3 6%	1 3%	1 3%	1 5%		2 5%
OPEN BEHAVIOUR	1 1%						– –
DISAGREEING	1 1%					1 3%	– –
ATTACKING						2 5%	– –
BLOCKING	9 9%	2 4%	7 23%	1 3%	3 16%	7 19%	4 9%
BRINGING IN	1 1%					2 5%	1 2%
SHUTTING OUT	12 12%	6 11%		4 13%	1 5%	6 16%	5 11%
Number of your individual contributions in each activity	$\frac{102}{396}$ (26%)	$\frac{52}{250}$ (21%)	$\frac{30}{390}$ (8%)	$\frac{34}{249}$ (14%)	$\frac{17}{145}$ (12%)	$\frac{36}{289}$ (13%)	$\frac{44}{287}$ (15%)
Number of contributions in the group in each activity (Average for group)	(59)	(36)	(56)	(35)	(21)	(41)	(41)

Figure 7.1 *Behaviour analysis profile for each individual*

statement can be made to the learners with similar objectives to the feedback in the interpersonal skills case. However, this will be more of an interim validation summary, as the learners would have been receiving skill etc feedback as their interview practices continued. An example of this interim summary is given in Figure 7.2.

This shows three interviews in which the individual observed was the interviewer during interview practices that were separated by feedback and input sessions. The percentages show that, although the total number of contributions made by the interviewer during an interview remained at about the same level, the type and value of the contributions changed significantly. In line with the training objectives, the proposing, giving information, disagreeing, attacking, blocking and shutting out behaviours all reduced, whereas the more positive behaviours for an interviewer (suggesting, building, seeking ideas and information, testing understanding and bringing in) all increased in a satisfactory manner. Initially the individual did not summarize; in the second interview this behaviour was used excessively by the interviewer; but by the third interview the lesson of having the interviewee perform the summaries had been learned well!

PRACTICAL TESTS AND DEMONSTRATIONS

These were described in Chapter 5 as initial assessment instruments, a practical demonstration being required of the learners to show the extent of their existing skill, and particular activities or tests set for this purpose. Interim testing of this nature can be performed in a very natural manner, with 'tests' after each progressive learning point being 'disguised' as practice opportunities for the learners, a form which is also a real opportunity to practise the learned skills.

This interim practical testing is particularly relevant in computer-based training programmes. If a new computer program is being introduced, the usual method is to do this in logical and progressive stages. After each stage it is perfectly normal for the learners to practise that stage, linked to the preceding ones, to demonstrate whether they have in fact learned – evaluation in a natural format. Remember the caveat given earlier about ensuring that you have time or other resource built into your programme to remedy any failings – you cannot be certain that your training will be 100 per cent effective for all the learners at any stage.

Category Interview	A	%	B	%	C	%
PROPOSING	8	18	3	8	1	2
SUGGESTING			1	3	1	2
BUILDING					4	9
SEEKING IDEAS			1	3	5	12
SEEKING INFORMATION	4	9	7	18	8	19
TESTING UNDERSTANDING			1	3	2	5
GIVING INFORMATION	12	27	7	18	6	14
DISAGREEING + REASONS	1	2	1	3	1	2
SUMMARIZING			4	10		
SUPPORTING	6	14	8	21	8	19
OPEN BEHAVIOUR					1	2
DISAGREEING	3	7	1	3		
ATTACKING	1	2	1	3		
BLOCKING	3	7				
BRINGING IN			2	5	6	14
SHUTTING OUT	6	14	2	5		
Number of your (Number of contributions in contributions each interview as a percentage)	44		39		43	

Figure 7.2 *Behaviour analysis profile one-to-one behaviours of an interviewer*

DIURNAL REVIEWS

In programmes that last longer than one day it is useful to have a daily assessment of some kind. This can serve three purposes:

1. acting as an interim evaluation of training effectiveness;
2. giving the learners the opportunity to consolidate their learning through the reflection necessary for the review;

3. allowing the learners to share their learning with others in the group and perhaps remind others of aspects that had slipped their minds.

There are several ways of approaching this review:

> - END OF THE DAY REVIEWS
> - BEGINNING OF THE DAY REVIEWS
> - WRITTEN AUDITS
> - VERBAL AUDITS
> - THREE-WORD REVIEWS
> - SPOT CHECKS

END AND BEGINNING OF THE DAY REVIEWS

The choice of approach causes frequent discussion among trainers, which rarely produces a universally acceptable result!

The principal arguments for reviewing at the end of the training day are:

- the learning is fresh in the learners' minds
- the learners are in the mode to make comments
- the review 'closes' the day neatly.

However, there are arguments against, and these include:

- immediate comment on learning does not necessarily mean this learning is significant;
- immediate recounting of learning may be too facile;
- the learners may be tired at the end of a training day and may say anything, simply to finish the review;
- the learners may be tired and may not be sufficiently bothered to make any comments;
- immediate feedback does not give the learners an opportunity to reflect and conclude;
- because the review is held at the end of the training day, there may be no (or insufficient) time to discuss the review items.

The alternative is to hold the review as the first activity of the following day's programme, having asked the learners to consider the day's events during the evening and overnight. The arguments against this include:

- the learners may not take sufficient time during the evening to reflect on and form conclusions about the training/learning;
- as a result of the time lapse, and minimal reflection, significant learning may not be recalled;
- the review may raise items requiring immediate resource and programme time – this may not be available;
- the review may raise requests of the trainers that they may not be able to deal with.

On the positive side:

- the learners should have had the opportunity to reflect and conclude on the learning of the day;
- if there are no training sessions during the evening on a residential course, the learners should have time to review;
- the items of learning included in the stated review, although they may not be all the ones the trainers have hoped for, will be those that have had an impact on the learners;
- there may be time for a more leisurely and considered review at the start of a day than at the end;
- more methods of review are possible than in an end of day review.

WRITTEN AUDITS OR REVIEWS

The more normal approach to reviews of this nature (whether held at the end or start of the day) is to ask the learners to reflect on the day's learning and write comments on this, either as an open response or in answer to specific questions. An example format for such a question-naire is given in Figure 7.3, which directs the learners to consideration of the training day, and asks them to complete the form at the end of the training day (for which sufficient time is given) or during the evening, for review the following morning.

If the questionnaires are completed at the end of the day they should be collected before the participants disperse so that you can consider the responses and take any necessary action in preparation for the following morning's session.

As the first activity the following morning the learning group, as one group or divided up (depending on the size of the full group), are led in a discussion of their responses. You will usually find that this

Please consider what has happened during today's training and answer the following questions. These responses, to the extent that you wish to do so, will be discussed at a review session tomorrow morning.

What have you learned today?
What helped that learning?
Was there anything that hindered this learning? If so, please describe it fully.
Was there anything on which you would have liked to have spent more time?
Was there anything on which you would have liked to have spent less time or had omitted?
Was there anything that you did not understand or agree with?

Figure 7.3 *Daily review questionnaire*

discussion can be quite extended, even if the learners have only positive comments to make. But it can obviously be even more extensive if there are problems that need to be discussed and remedied – that is what interim evaluation is all about!

VERBAL AUDITS OR REVIEWS

A verbal review can replace the written one if it is felt that the learners might not take kindly to written requirements. I feel that it is not as satisfactory as the discussion based on a written audit, because it lacks permanence, and writing down your views usually enables a clearer and more effective consideration.

However, if a verbal review is decided on, the list of questions in Figure 7.3 can be used as prompts to lead the discussion. A larger group of learners can be divided into smaller groups to discuss the questions before coming back together as the full group. This has the advantage of giving the quieter members the opportunity to have a say – this might be denied them by the very active contributors in the full group – and reports back can be made in a neutral way by a group spokesperson. This neutral approach is particularly useful to enable criticism to emerge if the critics do not feel they can verbalize their thoughts.

The verbal reporting can cause problems for you, but it is essential to let the learners see that you are taking notice of their views, by taking notes and making a response where necessary.

The three-word review

A simple but very effective form of daily audit, particularly in human relations programmes, can be the three-word review. At the start of the review, either at the end or at the start of the day (preferably the latter), ask the learners to write down three words or short phrases that describe their feelings at that stage about the training and the learning. When this has been done, invite the participants to call out their words or phrases. These should be entered, verbatim, on a flip-chart sheet. When they have all been entered a discussion might be started considering the words and why they were thought relevant, and taking or promising action wherever necessary. The learners can be invited to question the words used and the reasons behind them, and to challenge them as necessary. This discussion can be very lively, particularly during controversial programmes, but is usually very worthwhile.

SPOT CHECKS

Apart from perhaps the three-word review, the interim validations described here take a significant amount of time to perform, apart from any discussion or learning actions that may follow them. When time is limited, but it is desirable to take an interim audit of progress, there are shorter reviews that can be undertaken, although they cannot be as thorough as the more complex approaches.

These spot check approaches include:

> - THE THERMOMETER
> - THE SPEEDOMETER
> - HAPPY FACES
> - BLOBS
> - PROGRESSIVE BLOBS

In these spot checks the general activity by the group of learners is to identify their feelings or views at that stage of the programme, then make a mark of some kind on a prepared flipchart – these may be ticks, crosses or spots (the spots can be either drawn or, as self-adhesive spots, fixed to the chart). If you feel that there may be some reluctance on the part of the learners to indicate their views in front of the other learners (this in itself will be significant validation, particularly in an interactive skills event!), the flipchart can be turned round and the learners asked to come up one at a time.

In all the checks, look for clusters of spots – these indicate the majority views of the learners, or groups of learners. If the groups are quite separate in their recording, you will need to investigate the reasons for this division: sex or race differences; various departments or organizations; multi-discipline events; wide starting range and so on. Also look for individual ratings that differ considerably from the remainder – this raises a problem of possibly having to take some action for one individual, but tutorial approaches while the rest of the group is doing something else, or planned self-study, may produce results. Whatever the resultant action, it is necessary to speak to the individual, but not in front of the group, although identifying him or her may be unavoidable.

When all the marks have been made and any variations noted, the reasons for the significant variations have to be sought. This might mean the people who have made particular marks identifying themselves – with their permission, or making arrangements for a modified approach. Again the principal interim review caveat must be borne in mind – only embark on a review if you are able to satisfy identified problems.

The thermometer

As the title of this review suggests, you are attempting to take the 'temperature' of the learning group at a particular point in time. This temperature relates to how the learners are feeling about the event, its process and its progress since it started or since the last review.

Figure 7.4 shows the graphic that has been drawn on a flipchart sheet and is displayed at the beginning of the event, either facing towards or away from the group. In the example, the views of the learners about the event's atmosphere are sought, but a number of different views or feelings can be used instead. The learners are asked as individuals to come and make a personal mark (full initials, for example) at the 'temperature' they feel best represents how they view the programme. Any major divergences should be questioned, but no undue pressure should be put on a member to explain their views if they are reluctant to do so.

Figure 7.4 *The course atmosphere*

Usually, at the next stage the divergent member(s) volunteer to comment on their different opinions, if they still exist, or explain why they existed on the previous occasion.

The completed temperature chart can then be posted on the wall of the training room for later reference as necessary. At some other stage(s) in the event, and at the end, ask the members to enter their marks in the same way. Variations in the reception of the programme can then be monitored, visibly, and any problems dealt with as they arise or soon after. An effective time to have the diagram completed is immediately before the lunch break, rather than at the start or end of the day, or immediately after lunch! This also gives you time to consider the implications of the marks' positions..

The speedometer

One of the uses of the graphic shown in Figure 7.5 can be to enable the learners to show how they feel about the pace of the course, the speedometer obviously reflecting a car and its speed. Participants can enter their personal mark in the sector with which they identify,

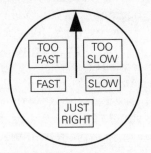

Figure 7.5 *The speed of the course*

Happy faces

A variation of the thermometer is to display on a chart a number of faces, with the mouths and expressions in progressive stages from smiling broadly to scowling or looking very miserable, as shown in Figure 7.6.

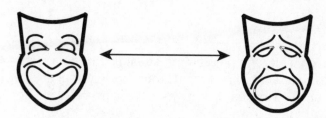

Figure 7.6   *Happy faces*

Such graphics are available on a number of computer programs, or self-adhesive faces can be purchased from stationers. The learners are asked to place a mark beside the face that best represents how they feel or, with self-adhesive faces, to place these on the chart. Again, this process can be repeated several times during the event to show the changes occurring and identify problems that need to be resolved.

Variations of the 'smiling' face can include the size of an open mouth to show how much the members feel they have the opportunity to participate.

Other uses

The three graphic reviews described above have been suggested as instruments to consider feelings about the event, the speed of the process and enjoyment or satisfaction with the programme. Of course, all the reviews can also be used to test interest, participation possibilities, usefulness, understanding, form of the event (too much x, too little y) – and so on.

THE 'BLOB' REVIEW

This is another instant form of progress review. The review itself can take a very short time, or can extend over about an hour or so – but time thus spent will be well worth it if you are unsure about how an event is progressing.

The short form of this review is very similar to the previous approaches. A pre-prepared flipchart can be exhibited showing the major elements of the event to that stage, or include questions about views on the training or learning that it is necessary to test. These might be very objective – for example, the learning points covered – or more reactive – seeking views on the learners' reactions to the programme. Figure 7.7 demonstrates an example of the reaction type of approach to the review.

Please consider the programme so far and place a blob – ● – in the box that you feel represents most closely your answer to the question. The boxes in between the extremes are for levels between these extremes.

Interesting	☐	☐	☐	☐	☐	☐	Boring
Clear	☐	☐	☐	☐	☐	☐	Confusing
Simple	☐	☐	☐	☐	☐	☐	Complicated
Time too short	☐	☐	☐	☐	☐	☐	Time too long
Visual aids good	☐	☐	☐	☐	☐	☐	Aids poor
Session should be retained	☐	☐	☐	☐	☐	☐	Session should be omitted
Learned a lot	☐	☐	☐	☐	☐	☐	Learned little
Confirmed usefully a lot	☐	☐	☐	☐	☐	☐	Confirmed little
Pace too fast	☐	☐	☐	☐	☐	☐	Pace too slow
Good interaction within group	☐	☐	☐	☐	☐	☐	Poor interaction within group
Good interaction with trainer	☐	☐	☐	☐	☐	☐	Poor interaction with trainer
Have no problems	☐	☐	☐	☐	☐	☐	Have lots of problems

Figure 7.7 *Blob review – reactionnaire type*

The learners are asked to go to the flipchart and put a pen mark or self-adhesive blob, ●, at the space on the scale representing their current views or feelings. The placement of these blobs will indicate the overall and individual views that may need to be discussed and taken into account by the trainer.

One variation to the two approaches mentioned above is to ask each learner to consider three significant statements they would like to make about the programme so far and to write these clearly and briefly on a flipchart or whiteboard at the front of the group. When all the statements have been written, the learners are asked to make their mark or place their blobs against the statements with which they agree. Commonly agreed views will soon become evident from the clustering, as will severely individual ones – the 'owners' of the latter might be invited to comment on their entries (without any challenge or value judgement being expressed or implied).

Progressive blob reviews

A major variation of the straightforward blob activity is to:

1. Ask each individual to write down three significant statements that they would like to make about the programme so far.
2. Divide the learning group into pairs to decide from the six statements they have brought to the meeting which three they wish to carry forward.
3. When the three statements have been decided upon, groups of four should be formed, with the similar brief of deciding on three statements from the six brought to the group.
4. If time and numbers permit, groups of eight can then be formed to decide on six statements to be the final agreed comments.
5. The six final statements should be entered on a chart similar to the one shown in Figure 7.8, and any clarification necessary made by the originators of the statements. The columns can be headed 'SD' = strongly disagree; 'D' = disagree; 'A' = agree; 'SA' = strongly agree with the statement.
6. All the members should then come to the chart and place a blob in the column relating to the rating with which they agree.

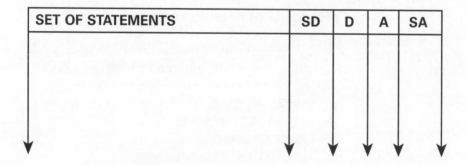

SET OF STATEMENTS	SD	D	A	SA

Figure 7.8   *'Blob' validation chart*

Once all the views have been entered, a pattern will emerge about the views of the learning group that will indicate if there are any problems that require immediate action.

SESSION REVIEWS

It is sometimes necessary for the trainer to assess the progress of the programme in a more detailed manner than is the case in a day's training and learning. Particularly in the longer and more complex types of programme, it may be too much to ask learners to add extensive reflection to their other difficulties. In such cases reviews of individual sessions or groups of associated sessions and activities can be conducted. These reviews have to be approached carefully as far as their coverage and timing are concerned. Very frequently different parts of a programme, although appearing separate are interrelated, and if the earlier sessions are reviewed, this may be done in isolation. Consequently the learners' responses may be negative because they have not yet had the benefit of the further material. There is no problem if the session or group of sessions are self-contained, and the review is only directed to these. Often on a training programme a day's training has a single theme – this is a useful link with the previously described end of day review – and the review can concentrate on this. The session review becomes more difficult for the learners if a day's training with a number of separate session groups is being considered. In this case it may be more effective to conduct the reviews following each discrete group.

You must consider seriously before introducing this type of review what type of feedback is required, why it is required and what you are going to do with the responses. There is little point in collecting information for collection's sake.

The form of session reviews

Session or group session reviews can take a number of forms, similar in many ways to the end of day review, and can include:

- VERBAL REVIEWS
- SIMPLE WRITTEN REVIEWS
- REACTIONNAIRES
- TICK-LIST QUESTIONNAIRES
- JUSTIFIABLE QUESTIONNAIRES

Verbal reviews

As we have seen earlier, these are probably the most difficult to conduct so that everybody has their say and everything that should be said is in fact said, but they often require the least time to plan and conduct.

Simple written reviews

These have also been considered in the end of day reviews, relevant questions being posed to enable as many appropriate responses as possible to emerge. These types of review are frequently based on the reactionnaire approach, which is concerned with the learners' reactions to the training as opposed to the extent of their learning. This subject will be considered in more depth in the next chapter, but the approach usually takes one of two forms – textual responses to text questions (the simple written reviews referred to earlier are examples of this) and reactionnaires requiring the learner to tick or ring a scale. A typical example of the latter type is shown in Figure 7.9.

SESSION: THE MANAGEMENT CYCLE

Please consider the session that has just ended and circle the scoring number that you feel represents most closely your answer to the question.

Interesting	6	5	4	3	2	1	Boring
Clear	6	5	4	3	2	1	Confusing
Simple	6	5	4	3	2	1	Complicated
Time too short	6	5	4	3	2	1	Time too long
Visual aids good	6	5	4	3	2	1	Aids poor
Session should be retained	6	5	4	3	2	1	Session should be omitted
Learned a lot	6	5	4	3	2	1	Learned little
Confirmed usefully a lot	6	5	4	3	2	1	Confirmed little

Figure 7.9 *A session reactionnaire*

The tick-list alternative is shown in Figure 7.10.

SESSION: THE MANAGEMENT CYCLE

Please consider the session that has just ended and place a tick in the space that you feel represents most closely your answer to the question. The spaces in between the extremes are for levels between these extremes.

Interesting	⌊_⌊_⌊_⌊_⌊_⌊	Boring
Clear	⌊_⌊_⌊_⌊_⌊_⌊	Confusing
Simple	⌊_⌊_⌊_⌊_⌊_⌊	Complicated
Time too short	⌊_⌊_⌊_⌊_⌊_⌊	Time too long
Visual aids good	⌊_⌊_⌊_⌊_⌊_⌊	Aids poor
Session should be retained	⌊_⌊_⌊_⌊_⌊_⌊	Session should be omitted
Learned a lot	⌊_⌊_⌊_⌊_⌊_⌊	Learned little
Confirmed usefully a lot	⌊_⌊_⌊_⌊_⌊_⌊	Confirmed little

Figure 7.10 *A session reactionnaire (tick list)*

Briefly, the arguments against the tick-list reactionnaire, apart from the general arguments against reactionnaires, are that:

- the approach is too simple and consequently is limited;
- a minimum amount of information emerges;
- this scoring can appear impersonal to the learners and therefore off-putting;
- scores can be given with little or no thought;
- less than honest or accurate responses may result.

Justifiable questionnaires

These are similar to the tick-list questionnaires but, instead of asking simply for a tick or a ring, comments are sought in order to try to have the completers justify their ratings. Obviously this requires more consideration by the learners about their ratings, and consequently the review should be:

- more accurate and considered;
- more comprehensive.

The tick-list questionnaire can be simply modified to the justified example by including a space that asks for specific comments about the rating. Many trainers complain that they rarely receive comments; most often this is because a space is left for comments with no further instructions. The learners must be specifically asked to comment in addition to placing their marks. An example of this type of questionnaire, again principally based on reaction, is shown in Figure 7.11. Again more information will be found in the next chapter

---

SESSION: THE MANAGEMENT CYCLE

Please consider the session that has just ended and circle the scoring number that you feel represents most closely your answer to the question.

In addition, under every rating you give, please comment on the reasons why you have given that rating – these comments will be as important as the ratings.

Interesting	6 5 4 3 2 1	Boring

Why have you given this rating?

Clear	6 5 4 3 2 1	Confusing

Why have you given this rating?

Simple	6 5 4 3 2 1	Complicated

Why have you given this rating?

Time too short	6 5 4 3 2 1	Time too long

Why have you given this rating?

Visual aids good	6 5 4 3 2 1	Aids poor

Why have you given this rating?

Session should be retained	6 5 4 3 2 1	Session should be omitted

Why have you given this rating?

Learned a lot	6 5 4 3 2 1	Learned little

What have you learned? (rating 6–4)

Why have you only learned a little? (rating 3–1)

Confirmed usefully a lot	6 5 4 3 2 1	Confirmed little

Why have you given this rating?

Figure 7.11 *A justified session reactionnaire*

LEARNING LOG REVIEWS

Many activities found in training and development programmes have a number of uses – aids to learning, aids to recall, evaluation, building confidence, learner intersharing and so on. The Learning Log is no different, and has value in all these aspects of the programmes.

A Learning Log is an instrument in which learners record, during a training event, and afterwards, the learning points in those events that have been significant in their learning and which they want to record for recall purposes. For a training event, the log consists of an introductory, explanatory page followed by a number of sheets in sets of three, one set for each day of the training event.

Set-sheet 1 can be used by the learner instead of or in addition to any note sheets that might be made during the training day of interesting, useful or significant learning points. Set-sheet 2 is used by the learners to sort and summarize the points from sheet 1 that they particularly want to recall, perhaps adding references to handouts and other information. Set-sheet 3 is a mini-action plan, detailing from sheet 2 entries about learning that the learner particularly intends to implement and how etc this action will be taken. The various sheet 3s can eventually be used in the formulation of the final action plan.

The log is issued at the start of the learning event and Set-sheets 2 and 3 are completed during the evenings of the event, giving the learners an opportunity to reflect on the events of the day and their significance.

At the start of the following day, allocating about 45 minutes, the learning group can be divided into smaller groups of four to six in which each gives a short presentation based on their previous evening's log entries. The learners find that in addition to consolidating further their learning they are reminded of other learning points by hearing the presentations of their colleagues. At the same time the trainer receives feedback on what has been learned to that stage and can compare this with the anticipated learning from the programme objectives.

Figure 7.12 illustrates part of an exemplar Learning Log. A log would normally be contained in a ring-binder with the introductory page and title sheets followed by sets of three sheets for use on the course, the number of sets depending on the number of days of the event – a five-day event would have five sets of three pages.

A LEARNING LOG BOOK

KEEPING A LEARNING LOG

The objective of attending a learning event is to learn something you can use. A complex event can contain a number of ideas, concepts, activities, etc that you might wish to implement at work. It can be difficult, particularly over an extended period, to remember all that you considered, perhaps even some important points.

A Learning Log:

- gives you a permanent document in which to record these ideas as they occur;
- helps you at a later stage think about what you have experienced and learned, particularly the key ideas you want to retain;
- helps you consider at leisure which aspects you want to implement and how you are going to do this;
- is a reminder for you about your intentions when you get back to work;
- is a permanent record of your progress and development and of what you have learned.

If the other notes you may have taken and the handouts issued during the training programme are combined with this log, you have a full record of your training to which you can refer at any time.

Your Learning Log should be completed frequently during the event – preferably during periods which may be allocated for this purpose – or during the evening following the training day. Do not leave its completion any longer than this, otherwise there is the danger that some useful and/or important ideas or learning may be lost.

From your ongoing notes section, review these notes and select the ideas, techniques, suggestions, activities that you feel could be important or significant for you.

In the second section of the log, describe these selections in as much detail as necessary so that you will be able to recall them later.

In the third section, preferably with a priority listing, describe, from your list in the second section, what you are going to implement or otherwise take action on:

- *What* are you going to do?
- *How* are you going to implement or action it?
- *When and/or by when* are you going to implement it?
- *What* resources will you need?
- *Who* can or needs to be involved?
- *What* implications are there for effects on others?

Page 1

THE CONTINUED USE OF THE LEARNING LOG

On the training programme

At the start of the day following the one for which you have completed your log you will, in a small group, be asked to describe the entries you have made. This presentation will:

(a) help you clarify your thoughts on the area presented;
(b) help you in the recall process;
(c) widen the views of the remainder of the group who may not have seen the implications of the areas you have high-lighted;
(d) raise the opportunity for clarification of doubtful points.

As a continuous process

A Learning Log is not intended for use only on training pro-grammes. We are learning all the time, in every type of situation, and a log can help us capitalize on these opportunities. If you read a book and there are ideas that you want to remember and implement, enter these in the log. If, in discussion with others, ideas are suggested that you feel may be of use to you, remember them and enter them in your log at the first opportunity. Keep referring to your log constantly to remind you of activities that you have not yet implemented.

Your line manager, in his or her process of your continuing assessment, will not only find your log entries valuable in assessing your development, but could be impressed by your intent and persistence.

Remember that if eventually you decide to seek the award of the Training and Development National Vocational Qualification this record can form a useful part of the portfolio you will need to produce.

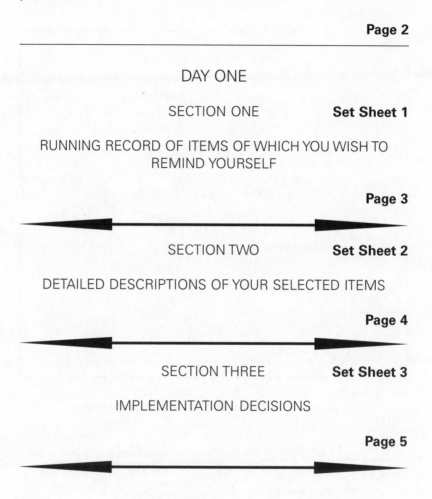

Figure 7.12 *A Learning Log*

An alternative Learning Log

Many trainers have been baffled that learners do not see a particular aid to learning as ideal as they do. This is usually because the aid is too complex, too long or too boring to appeal to them. The training adage KISS – Keep It Short and Simple – should be applied if this is the case because, although the Learning Log is an ideal aid to learning, if the learners do not use it, it is failing in its purpose.

If this occurs with the Learning Log described above, Figure 7.13 shows an alternative log.

LEARNING LOG
Course .... Date ....
Things I want to discuss
Things I want to know more about
Things I want to remember
Things to do

Figure 7.13 *An alternative Learning Log*

This log would be used in the same way as that already described, ie completed by the learners during and at the end of the training day, then discussed in small groups the following morning. Completion on a continuing basis after the training programme should also be encouraged.

8
—

Evaluation at the End of the Event – I

The purpose of training and development is to produce change (in knowledge, skills and attitudes) in the individuals from a level that is not acceptable for some reason – introduction of new work, remedial requirements, career development etc – to one that is acceptable to the organization. Validation and evaluation are used to demonstrate and assess these changes. Consequently when a training and development programme or package is completed, it is necessary to introduce some form of validation measures – usually a repeat of the tests and assessments used at the start of the programme (if indeed these were used).

Almost traditionally, most 'evaluation' stops at the end of a training course with the issue of some form of questionnaire about the course, usually what is unfortunately known as the 'happiness' sheet. This, if the previous actions and the end of programme investigations are valid, is better than nothing, but it is not evaluation. These limitations are no longer acceptable in today's climate of cost and value effectiveness and the increasing interest of senior management in training's commitment to these. The start of extended effectiveness of evaluation is a realistic end of programme validation that completes previously performed tests and assessment

GUIDELINES TO END OF PROGRAMME VALIDATION

Before we progress to the specific forms of validation that can be used with effect, some general guidelines include:

- Hand out the validation questionnaires well before the end of the event and allow sufficient time for them to be completed
- KISS – keep it as short and as simple as possible
- Explain the objectives of the validation
- Stress the importance of validation and evaluation
- Let the participants know what is going to happen to their responses
- Promise, if possible, a copy of the validation summary
- Don't try to influence the responses

Figure 8.1 *Guidelines for end of programme validation*

Allow sufficient time for the process to be completed

Do not, as is all too common, hand out any end of programme instruments two or three minutes before the end of the event and ask the learners to fill them in before they leave. Even worse is to hand the learners the instruments as they are actually leaving, asking them to send them back. The instruments should have been designed for maximum effectiveness, which will have taken valuable time. So, apart from anything else, their importance is reduced, or even negated by such offhand treatment.

Part of your design of any end of programme instruments will be an assessment of how long people would take to complete them effectively. This is the minimum time that should be allocated at the end of the training event, and should be part of the programme. In longer programmes this time allocation could be substantial – with completion of a questionnaire, an action plan and discussion of the latter, the time required at the end of a week-long course could be up to two hours, if not the final half-day.

KISS

Keep it short and simple as far as you can. The longer and more complicated the questionnaires you give to the learners – who after all will have at least half their minds on going home – the less likely you are to receive them realistically completed. There will, of course, be times when you will want and/or need to use longer and more complicated approaches, in which case the importance of the activity must be stressed and ample time allocated.

Make evaluation important to the learners

If the learners get the impression that you do not see evaluation as an important part of the training/learning cycle, they will reflect this lack of importance in the way they respond. Evaluation is important (especially the learners' part in it) and you can make this clear in your introduction. Let the learners know what you want them to do, and why; let them know what you will do with the responses and who will see them, or whether there will be an anonymous summary. If it is feasible (and there are few reasons why it should not be), promise the learners a copy of the results of the validation, for example a summary of the comments made by their group and, if there are problems, what you are going to do about these (more real recommendation is made for people to attend or not attend training programmes by word of mouth than by any other means).

Don't try to influence the responses

Your tests and questionnaires should be so designed that they give no indications of your personal preferences. They should relate to the learning and the training provided. Don't praise the learners insincerely in the hope that you may receive higher marks; the attempt may rebound if the learners see through your strategy, and if they don't they may in fact give higher scores than they believe in – this contaminates your evaluation and your clients and sponsors may question why, for example, training demand reduces for what appears to be a wonderful programme!

Having issued the questionnaires, don't peer over the learners' shoulders as they are completing them. Even though they know you are going to see them eventually, interference during completion can easily affect the responses.

NON-REPETITIVE VALIDATION

As we have seen earlier, pre- or start of programme action to test or otherwise assess the starting level of the learners is not always possible. This in effect means that, apart from programmes concerned with the introduction of completely new material (where there is no doubt that the learners are starting from zero knowledge and skills), realistic evaluation is difficult, if not impossible. After all, if you don't know where the learners have come from, you will not know how far they have progressed as a result of the training. This statement is not absolute, but any claims for evaluation made with no before and after measurement must be viewed with suspicion.

However, remember that these constraints do not apply if no pre-testing was undertaken because it was known categorically that the learners would have no knowledge or skill in the area included in the programme. In effect there is a pre-learning measurement – zero – and any validation showing that learning has occurred is an increase over this zero point.

In such cases, the tests and other forms of assessment described in Chapters 4, 5 and 6 can be used as end of programme validation instruments. It may be necessary to make the instruments rather more substantial than you might otherwise have done, in order to ensure that you have evidence of as wide a learning as possible within the objectives of the training.

END OF PROGRAMME VALIDATION INSTRUMENTS

If you are attempting validation from the zero base, or as a repeat of the pre- or start of programme tests and assessments, the following lists summarizes the possible approaches:

- Knowledge – usually, but not always, written tests
- Skills – operating or procedural
- Skills by means of a practical demonstration test and more general ones that will be assessed by activity and process
- Observation of the learners performing a task, real or simulated; can be preceded by a written knowledge test
- Attitudes and behaviour – usually practical, observational approaches

Knowledge tests and practical demonstrations

In most cases it is ideal, and usually practicable, to repeat the test or demonstration requirement as it was posed at the start of the programme. The test or scored demonstration results can then be compared directly with the earlier ones, showing in as objective a manner as possible the changes over the training period. If the training has been continuous or not open to contamination in other ways, the improvement shown by the change can be fairly readily attributed to the training.

Observation of general skills

Assessment of more subjective learning aspects can also be approached in similar ways to the earlier attempts to assess. In, for example, negotiation skills training, the first series of practice negotiations were observed and assessed. Subsequent training put forward skills and techniques in negotiation and the final series of negotiations, when observed using the same criteria for the earlier series, should demonstrate to what extent the participants have taken from the learning points what they should have done according to the accepted model and the course objectives. These results will obviously be more subjective and less complete than practical demonstrations and knowledge tests, but if the approaches are kept as consistent as possible, a reasonable degree of comparison is possible.

Observation of behavioural learning

Where the emphasis of the training and learning has been on behavioural, interactive and interpersonal skills, an instrument similar to Behaviour Analysis will probably have been used during the event. Consequently a progressive bank of behavioural data will have been collected.

At a critical point in the learning event, say about two-thirds of the way through a week's course on interactive skills, it is useful to feed back the data to that point to the learners so that they can assess the broad image of their behaviour during the event. Following this, plans are usually made for some form of behaviour modification by the learners, and the subsequent and final behaviour observations will demonstrate for the learners and the trainer to what extent they have been successful in applying the learning and the modification plans.

Figure 7.1 in Chapter 7 demonstrates one example of the data summary that can be supplied to the learners on an interpersonal skills course as staged feedback to enable them to make modification plans. If necessary, this format can be updated at the end of the event to show the changes made following the intermediate plans.

A number of analyses can be produced from the data in Figure 7.1, which shows the behaviour pattern for an individual over a number of activities. The figures show that the person contributed to the group discussions initially at a higher rate than the group average – eg in Activity A the person contributed 102 of the group's 396 total contributions (the group average being 59), a rate of 26 per cent; and in Activity B a contribution of 52 of the group's 250 total contributions (the group average equalling 36), a rate of 21 per cent. By the time the programme had progressed to Activity F, our individual's rate had decreased to 13 per cent with 36 contributions out of the group's 289 (group average equalling 41). The overall impression is that the individual was starting to control him- or herself much more in the group situation and not making the lion's share of the contributions.

However, the total number of contributions is only part of the story, and it is necessary to examine the specific behaviours to gain a more effective appreciation of any change. This examination shows that although the total contributions had changed by decreasing, there was little difference in the particular behaviours, and in fact some demonstrated a less than desirable pattern. This pattern suggests that about half, and sometimes considerably more, of the contributions are simply statements by the individual of their views, opinions and knowledge, at the expense of building a relationship with others and finding out what they feel – a self-centred approach within the group. This is suggested by the overall 50 per cent rate for giving information, 9 per cent blocking behaviour and 11 per cent shutting others out to make some of these statements. This compares with the 11 per cent rate of seeking the views of others, 5 per cent supporting behaviour, only 2 per cent bringing in others, and virtually no building supportively on the proposals made by others. The 5 per cent rate of proposals suggests that, although the individual has a lot to say, little of this comes out in a creative, constructive form of proposals for action.

Obviously a chart of this nature cannot give all the information necessary for a complete behavioural picture, but it does at least give a factual basis for the start of a discussion and analysis by the individuals. This is not an easy process, as charts have to be prepared from the activity behaviour observations for each participant, but it serves the dual purpose of feeding back a lot of information to the learners and at the same time assessing their progress towards the desired change.

GROUP REVIEWS

Verbal and written group reviews were described in Chapter 7 when interim, diurnal reviews were considered. These approaches can be replicated as end of programme reviews, the brief taken by the group or groups being to review and comment on the event/programme as a whole. The groups can be given an open brief to comment on whatever they feel is significant, or can be posed specific questions. In many ways the former is preferable, because the subjects they select, positive or negative, will be the ones that are important to them. However, they may not comment comprehensively or on areas that it is particularly desirable for a review to be made; it is only with prescriptive questions that this range of coverage can be obtained.

The group approach to review can be considered one of the least effective of methods as so many aspects can contaminate the responses – end of course fatigue or euphoria; thoughts only on going home; over-contribution by some members and under- or non-contribution by some; comments selected on the basis of pleasing/displeasing the trainer and so on. However, there are occasions when this will be the most relevant method of obtaining validation views and at least, when the groups are in the discussion period, there will be a sharing of views with some possible consequent learning.

REACTIONNAIRES AND QUESTIONNAIRES

The majority of end of programme validations are obtained by one or both of these approaches. The basic difference between them is that the reactionnaire obtains (whether this was intended or not) the reactions, views, feelings and personal opinions of the learners to a range of features of the programme (reflecting customer satisfaction more than anything else), whereas the questionnaire in effective validation concentrates on the learning aspects and attempts to quantify or at least justify the responses. The 'happiness' sheet so frequently referred to in training circles is a poor example of a reactionnaire which is usually biased so that the responses are always in the good to excellent area, or otherwise tend to reflect the learners' euphoria at the end of a course. They may of course reflect the opposite, which may or may not have anything to do with the effectiveness of the course, but rather are personal attitudes because of the type of training or even interactions with the trainer. Of course, if a 'bad' review of this nature is produced by all or most of the learners, it certainly gives an indication that something, albeit undefined, was wrong on the programme.

The valid type of reactionnaire seeks to obtain responses about important aspects of the programme, and in particular those concerned with the learning. Of course it may be said that questions and responses about the comfort of the hotel; the facilities of the conference centre; the extent to which the participants 'enjoyed' the event, may have an influence on the learning, but in themselves they are not concerned with validation of the learning itself. By all means, if it is desirable that information of this nature is required, ask relevant questions, but remember that they are not directly concerned with the validation of the learning.

The limitations of reactionnaires

Accepting that reactionnaires are used extensively by trainers, often without their realizing their diminished value in evaluation, we must recognize their limitations. These include that they do the following:

- give only a very limited indication of learning and usually fail either to justify or quantify the extent of learning;
- give little indication of the transfer of the learning to the work environment and the likelihood of its implementation;
- give no real measure of the extent of the learning although, with their 'tick boxes' and scoring approaches, give every indication of being a mathematically based approach (the ticked scores can be analysed in a number of ways, but the subjective base of the figures does not enable an objective result, however much it may appear to do so);
- can be completed with little thought, especially if tick boxes alone are provided;
- provide at most an impression of what the learners *think* they have learned.

The value of reactionnaires

Although reactionnaires are generally subjective, rough and ready means of obtaining views on a wide range of aspects of the event from a programme's participants, they are not sufficiently precise to act as evaluation instruments. However, they have their uses and indeed, value. These can be summarized as:

- If responses are favourable, they can provide useful material for programme publicity by the use of the quasi-arithmetical analyses possible.
- They provide information about the subjective views of the learners, perhaps the highest level of views that can be obtained for some programmes – remember the criteria that objective training should be capable of objective measurement; subjective level training can only be assessed by subjective means.
- They can provide a warning signal where something has gone badly wrong in a programme, this being demonstrated by the reactive feelings of the participants.
- If broad objectives have been stated at the beginning of the programme by the learners, the broad brush of the reactionnaire can be used to test the satisfaction of these objectives.
- Responses to questions seeking useful reactive data can be sought in this way – how effectively the training need was identified; whether there was a pre-course briefing and views on its effectiveness; environmental factors that worked against full learning during the event; programme design that the learners could identify as unhelpful; the acceptability or otherwise (as opposed to value) of the learning methods used and so on. It must always be appreciated, however, that you are seeking subjective views which may be given without a knowledge base for comparison, and the opinions do not represent a measure of real value. But, if a learner makes a statement, that is their view, the significance of which is magnified if a number of similar responses are made.
- They demonstrate, particularly in out-of-organization courses, the important aspect of customer satisfaction with the training and development programmes.

Obviously the value of a reactionnaire increases if the approach is improved beyond the simple tick list, with the opportunity afforded to the learners to justify their scorings, comment fully on these scorings, compare and contrast levels of information and so on. But, in the end, the responses are views, feelings and opinions only, and must be seen as such in an overall assessment. Unfortunately, on too many occasions, a tick list, happiness sheet is accepted as realistic validation of a programme (usually if it supports the programme, but decried as subjective if it does not!).

PROBLEMS IN CONSTRUCTING REACTIONNAIRES (AND SOME SOLUTIONS)

Avoid being haphazard

The major problem, or fault, in the construction of reactionnaires is a haphazard approach to the questions. Because of the little-value happiness sheet approach, questions are often included only because the designer feels they should be, or because they are his or her favourite questions. The questions must be related directly to the specific training programme and must have relevance – for example, it may be interesting to find out whether the learners enjoyed the programme, but did this 'enjoyment' contribute to any learning achieved? Sometimes learning is only achieved with accompanying 'pain', in which case the response may not reflect enjoyment.

Multiple questions

The learners will experience difficulty in answering and the analyser difficulty in understanding the responses to multiple questions. An example of this might be:

How do you rate the level of the visual aids and the handouts?

Low   1   2   3   4   5   6   7   High

To which question will the response relate, particularly if, say, the visual aids were good but the handouts poor? If only one answer is given, on which aspect is the responder commenting?

Define the words

There can be a problem in defining the words used. If the question is posed with a tick-list scale as shown below, what do the responses mean?

What did you think of the visual aids used?

Very good   7   6   5   4   3   2   1   Poor

Do 'good' and 'poor' relate to their artistic qualities, to their relevance, to their level of clarity, or to something else? Are *all* the visual aids commented on? How can the analyser correlate the interpretation of 'very good' or 'poor' or some level between, one responder with another? These are not pedantic points, but examples of real problems you may encounter.

Consistency of scoring polarity

This can take two forms. One is the transposition from one question to another of the position of the scoring poles; the other the transposition of the scoring numbers. An example of the first might be:

1. How well do you rate the visual aids used?

    Very good   7   6   5   4   3   2   1   Poor

2. How well do you rate the handouts issued?

    Poor   1   2   3   4   5   6   7   Very good

3. How interesting did you find the practical activities?

    Very   1   2   3   4   5   6   7   Not at all

Note that in question 2 the 'very good' and 'poor' poles have been reversed from their positions in question 1 and, in question 3, the scoring figures have been reversed. One argument used in support of this is that the transpositions make the completers read the reactionnaire more carefully. In my experience what usually happens is that the completers ignore the transpositions and place their ticks towards the pole they used for the first question. In order to avoid any possibility of this, stick to a standard listing.

Avoid loading the questions

Another feature that questions 1 and 2 above highlight is the loaded nature of questions. This is a tactic that should be avoided (although it is frequently practised), since the learners are led to a biased answer rather than a completely neutral one. The questions are asking 'how *well*' the learner rates, suggesting that the answers are simply levels of 'well'. An unloaded version of these questions would simply omit the word 'well'.

Immediacy

You must be certain that questions relating to immediacy are in fact about aspects that have an immediate application. For example, if handouts are given out on a course for use by the learners after the course, the following question asks the learners questions about use that can only be assessed after the course, when the learning has been applied back at work.

How useful do you think the handouts are going to be?

Very useful   7   6   5   4   3   2   1   Not useful

Consistency

Although it is not always possible, you should try to maintain consistency of rating levels. If the questions posed vary considerably and frequently between how often, how much, to what extent, what was good, indicate the extent and so on – although this varies the question and may make the reactionnaire less boring – the completer can be confused by the different forms of question. Avoid the possibility of this by making your questions as consistent and relevant as possible.

Antonyms

A common failing is not to make the options at the poles of the scale antonyms. The vagaries of the English language sometimes make these distinctions rather confused, but, for example, 'bad', not 'poor' is the antonym of 'good'. Frequently used antonyms in polarized scales include:

Very much – very little; Good – bad; Excellent – poor (but also Rich – poor); Very often – not at all; Frequently – rarely; and so on.

The principal problem, however, in the construction of reactionnaires remains the risk of making them 'happiness' sheets which can be quickly completed, with the learner simply running down a tick list, giving the responses little if any thought – either ticking all the 'good/bad' spaces or randomly placing the ticks. The most effective remedy for this is that, in addition to completing a tick box, the learner should be asked specific questions to justify the scoring given. Frequently the tick box is followed by a line space prefaced by 'Comments' – only too often there are no entries in these spaces when the reactionnaires are handed in, usually too late for the trainer to ask any questions of clarification. Always include ample space for comments and, if specific questions cannot be posed, draw the learners' attention to the requirement to make comments to justify their scorings. This reduces the euphorically completed reactionnaire, since the constant 'good' rater will be made to think and state why they consider 'good' the most relevant rating.

THE TYPICAL 'HAPPY' SHEET

A typical 'happy' sheet is reproduced as Figure 8.2, showing the general nature of the questions in these cases. You will note that not only are the questions very general, but they are not separated into types and are generally selected from questions to which good responses are usually obtained. The scales of response are not consistent and the words describing them are designed, even in the worst scenario, not to be damning.

Finally, it is simply a tick list that can be completed in a minute, with little or no consideration of the responses.

Please consider the following questions and ring the scale number that you feel represents most closely your views.

1. How interesting did you find the course?

   Very   5   4   3   2   1   Not too interesting

2. How much new information did you acquire?

   Quite a lot   5   4   3   2   1   Not too much

3. How would you rate the following:

	Good	Fair	Poor
Content of the sessions?	3	2	1
The hotel?	3	2	1
Sequence of the sessions?	3	2	1
The trainers?	3	2	1
The seating arrangements?	3	2	1
The videos shown?	3	2	1
The visual aids?	3	2	1
The course overall?	3	2	1

Figure 8.2 *A typical 'happy sheet' reactionnaire*

THE SPECIFIC FORM OF REACTIONNAIRE

More to the point, and usually more helpful, is the specific reactionnaire that seeks information about participants' views on certain aspects of the programme's environment.

HOTEL ACCOMMODATION

Ring the score you wish to record

BEDROOM COMFORT

Good   7   6   5   4   3   2   1   Poor

WHY HAVE YOU GIVEN THIS SCORE?

....

....

BEDROOM FACILITIES

Good   7   6   5   4   3   2   1   Poor

WHY HAVE YOU GIVEN THIS SCORE?

....

....

MEALS QUALITY

Good   7   6   5   4   3   2   1   Poor

WHY HAVE YOU GIVEN THIS SCORE?

....

....

TRAINING ACCOMMODATION

Good   7   6   5   4   3   2   1   Poor

WHY HAVE YOU GIVEN THIS SCORE?

....

....

Figure 8.3 *Specific form of reactionnaire*

In Figure 8.3 this is the hotel used for the training course. Although this questionnaire is seeking reactions and views and is not concerned directly with validating the learning, it is made more effective by asking specific questions and, further, is seeking justification of these comments.

THE BLANK SHEET QUESTIONNAIRE

This type of questionnaire can be considered a half-way house between the reactionnaire and the validation questionnaire, as it gives the participants the opportunity to make comments overall. As the name implies, it is basically a blank sheet of paper on which the learners are asked to make any comments they wish about the training programme. No direction is given and, in fact, is not desirable, as it could contaminate the responses. The learners will comment on those aspects of the programme that were significant or important to them, and consequently you will – in theory at least – receive the comments they really want to make.

TRAINING PROGRAMME REVIEW

In the space below please enter as many comments as you wish to make about the training programme you have just completed. Feel free to comment on any aspect of the programme. Please add your name and the date at the end of your comments.

Figure 8.4 *Blank sheet questionnaire*

The major problem with this approach is that the comments will be very mixed in terms of the programme – they may include reactions and comments on learning – and you have no control over what the learners comment on. Obviously, if there are areas on which you want specific comments, this is not the most appropriate type of approach.

Analysis of the responses is equally difficult, although the responses can be summarized and scrutinized for common comments. If there has been something particularly good or bad, there will usually be more than one comment.

THE FEELINGS REACTIONNAIRE

The interpersonal or interactive behavioural programme must rate as one of the most subjective forms of training and development, and as such is very difficult to assess objectively. The use of activity and behaviour analysis has been discussed as assessment approaches that are as close to objective measurements as possible in this area. With the comments about reactionnaires in general in mind, a reactionnaire for an interpersonal skills programme will be purely subjective reaction. Tick lists are not very relevant and are frequently rejected by the learning group as alien to this form of learning. One suggestion is not to be overly concerned about the subjectivity debate, and accept subjective assessments for subjective subjects. After all, you have probably bent your knee at the throne of near objectivity by using behaviour analysis!

Figure 8.5 is an example of a reactionnaire that might be used at the end of such an event as it concentrates on the feelings held by the learners who have experienced a programme which has majored to a large extent on feelings.

Please comment, in the spaces provided, your feelings about the subject raised by the question. Comment as freely as you wish.

1. The major feelings I have at the moment about this event are ....
....
2. If this course had been a film, book or play, the title would have been ....
3. The parts of the event I enjoyed most were ....
4. The parts of the experience I can make most use of are ....
5. Something I learned, or had usefully confirmed about myself, was
....
6. Something I learned, or had usefully confirmed about other people, was ....
7. The parts of the event that I enjoyed least were ....
8. The parts of the event that I can make least use of were ....
9. If I were starting this experience again I would ....
10. One thing I regret having done during the event was....................
11. One thing I regret not having done was...
12. Right now I am feeling ....

Figure 8.5 *Feelings review*

Because of the open nature of the questions, in addition to their subjective nature, this type of reactionnaire is very difficult to summarize and review. Perhaps the only action is to produce a textual report grouping as far as possible similar (or different) responses.

SELF-REPORTING REVIEWS – THE THREE-TEST

The three-test was introduced briefly in Chapter 6, and a typical review questionnaire was included as Figure 6.7. The introduction of the three-test came about because when I was trying to assess and evaluate interpersonal and interactive skills programmes, I found that the simple pre- and post-test used mainly in practical programmes were not relevant in the more subjective forms of training. These included inter-personal and interactive skills courses, and certain aspects of general management skills training where the emphasis is on dealing with people or some form of human relations – negotiation, leadership, supervision, management of people, interviewing and the like. Because of their nature, other than activity analysis, they depended to a major extent on the subjective, albeit experienced observations of the trainer and self-assessment approaches.

The problem with the pre- and post-test approach is that in a practical situation it is obvious, usually by simple observation, whether the learner can or cannot perform an operation, or to what degree on a scorable scale.

In more general activities such as negotiation skills, the assessment by observation frequently depends on opinion rather than hard fact, thus reducing the objectivity. When we are considering these general skills and the even more subjective ones of people development, because of this reduced or absence of fully objective tests, the results of any attempt at pre- and post-testing become merely estimates. This uncertainty is increased by the fact that asking learners at the start of such events to assess their own skills must suffer somewhat because the learners may not know in which areas they are deficient. It may not be until they have completed the training process that they realize the limitations they had at the start!

Self-assessment in practice

A self-assessment reactionnaire such as the one shown in Figure 6.7 as the pre-test instrument might include a question about the learner's awareness of the behaviour modification they need to do.

	High									Low
12 Being aware of what behaviour modification I need to do	10	9	8	7	6	5	4	3	2	1

At the start of the course the self-assessment by a learner might be at the scale point 7, the learner describing him- or herself as very, although not completely aware of their failings and their behaviour modification needs.

The same test instrument is used at the end of the course in an attempt to 'measure' the changes that the learner was able to self-assess. On this occasion, the learner might give a rating of 8, indicating that they felt that their awareness had increased during the course and that now, although not complete, their awareness is much more significant. Taking into account that comparison is subjective and not strictly arithmetical, this suggests that there has been an increase in awareness of about 10 per cent. This is not an exceptional increase bearing in mind the training and learning opportunities offered, but if we look back at the pre-test we see that the initial scoring was 7, a not insubstantial level of awareness. However, the subjectivity and self-assessment do raise suspicions about the initial assessment. To what extent was there some self-delusion in this initial statement, a suspicion that might be supported by the facilitator's observations during the event and the more objective evidence of behaviour analysis?

The third element of the three-test

One method of reducing this contamination of the results, and attempting to assess more accurately the amount of change, is to introduce the third element of the three-test. After the self-assessment reaction-naire has been completed for the second time at the end of the training event, the learners are asked to complete the same instrument for a third time. Comments should be made on the possible contaminatory aspects and that this is an attempt to determine the real level of change. However, on this third occasion the learners are asked to complete the reactionnaire as if they were doing so at the start of the programme, *but with their current perception of their skills* – in other words, knowing what they know now.

The results of this third completion can fall within a wide range, depending on the real awareness of the learner (at both the start and finish of the programme), their level of self-deception or self-delusion, and so on. Let us take the example of the learner who has previously rated 7 then 8, and who rates their awareness score for this question as 3. This considerably lower revised starting score may be a truer estimate of their skill at that pre-training stage. As a result, the percentage learning change (now 3 to 8) is seen as an increase of 50 per cent, a much more worthwhile value for expensive training and a realistic validation of the content, etc for at least that learner. Some may even revise their initial awareness to 1 or 2, the increase to 8 thus representing a substantial amount of change over the training programme and an indication of its true value and validity for such learners.

Figure 8.6 shows the summary of the reactionnaires for an individual learner – the results can of course be aggregated to show a full course's change. The figures show that when the end of programme assessments are compared with the revised start of programme scores (the 'real' initial ratings), there has been a substantial increase in some categories, no change in others, and even reductions in one or two. This is a typical result, although there can be considerable variation between the members of a learning group.

The first 'Column' gives the self-rating on the first completion of the reactionnaire; the second 'Column' the self-rating at the end of the programme; and the third 'Column' the revised rating for how the learner should have been at the beginning of the programme. The figures in parentheses under the second 'Column' are the percentage increases if the initial rating had been correct; those under the third 'Column' are the corrected changes as a result of the recompleted starting assessment.

The final percentage changes show that, of the 18 categories self-assessed, there has been an improvement over the course in 15 categories, ranging from +20 per cent to +80 per cent, making a total change over all the categories of 82 per cent. This compares with an improvement in 14 categories from +10 to +70 per cent from a total change of 35 per cent as assessed using the original initial assessments.

In the final assessment one category hasn't changed, the learner reassessing at a higher level than originally and equating this with the end of learning level – this suggests that the learner was very aware of their listening skills and in fact discovered that they were even better than they had thought.

In two categories the final assessment showed awareness of two behavioural skills lower than the reviewed initial level, by 10 per cent in each case. In the one relating to awareness of being brief and concise, this apparent anomaly can be explained from the course itself, showing the figures do not necessarily tell the full story. The learner started at a level of 8 – this figure was confirmed by the review, but finished at a level of 7. However, during the course the learner was required to look

CATEGORY	COLUMN 1	COLUMN 2	COLUMN 3
In the group as member of the group	(Initial)	(Terminal)	(Revised initial)
1 Being aware of my own behaviour	6	8 (+20)	2 (+60)
2 Being aware of the behaviour of others	8	9 (+10)	2 (+70)
3 Being aware of the reactions of others to my behaviour	7	8 (+10)	3 (+50)
4 Being aware of my reaction to the behaviour of others	6	8 (+20)	1 (+70)
5 Being aware of how much I talk	9	9 (0)	2 (+70)
6 Being brief and concise	8	7 (–10)	8 (–10)
7 Being aware of how much I support others	6	8 (+20)	9 (–10)
8 Always explaining my disagreements	8	7 (–10)	4 (+30)
9 Being aware of how much I build on the ideas of others	1	5 (+40)	1 (+40)
10 Sensing the feelings of others	7	8 (+10)	1 (+70)
11 Being aware of how much I interrupt others	6	9 (+30)	1 (+80)
12 Being aware of how much I really listen to others	7	9 (+20)	9 (0)
13 Telling others what my feelings are	4	8 (+40)	2 (+60)
14 Being aware of what behaviour modification I need to do	6	9 (+30)	5 (+40)
15 Knowing how to modify my behaviour	1	8 (+70)	1 (+70)
16 Being aware of how much I bring out the views of others	3	8 (+50)	6 (+20)
17 Being positive	8	8 (0)	2 (+60)
18 My general overall level of my interpersonal skills	7	9 (+20)	2 (+70)

Figure 8.6 *Summary of three-test responses*

at a number of other changes and as a result tended to ignore this particular behaviour. In the case of support of others, the learner having progressed through the course, realized that he/she was better at supporting others than they had originally thought. But again because they concentrated on improving other behaviours, the support aspect was allowed to slip, in fact by practising the difficult behaviour of building on others' proposals, explaining disagreements and reducing the amount of interrupting, among others.

The apparent (or real) anomalies need to be examined with the learner before being able to consider the real reasons, rather than the ones assumed by a drop in skill. Other changes may need to be queried, and compared with, say, behaviour analyses to ensure that the full picture of change emerges.

My experience has been that the three-test produces more realistic (not necessarily 'better') results than the pre or post-test in appropriate learning programmes. The three-test also compares well with other assessments, such as behaviour analysis made during the programme. However, it must be recognized that the method is still sensitive to subjective treatment, which of course is found in any form of self-assessment other than direct, practical testing.

9

—

Evaluation at the End of the Event – 2

Methods for validating or assessing the training programme were discussed in Chapter 8. These included the common approach of using a reactionnaire but making this more valuable and realistic as a validation instrument by seeking comments in addition to having a simple tick list. These methods, however, still fall short of an effective validation of the objectives' achievements of both the training and development programme and the learners. In this chapter question-naires and action plans are discussed as more effective instruments of validation and evaluation than reactionnaires, although there is often value in supplementing them with a well-constructed reactionnaire, particularly:

- in the case of the first two or three courses of a new programme;
- if an existing programme starts to have undefined problems.

My concept of a 'questionnaire' is an instrument that concentrates on validating the training programme and the learners' objectives through an investigation, via the learners, of the learning achieved and their intentions of implementation. A properly constructed and administered questionnaire should be able to stand up to scrutiny and answer the basic question that will be posed by interested senior and line manage-ment, 'Am I getting my money's worth from your training? – Prove it!'

VALIDATION QUESTIONNAIRES

Questionnaires are of course generic instruments and are used for a variety of purposes and in a range of forms, some of which appear very close to the foregoing descriptions of reactionnaires. My description of a questionnaire in the validation and evaluation of training is an instrument that defines the amount and range of learning achieved by a learner within a training programme, and one that can also identify the reasons why (some) learning did not occur. Notice that the emphasis all the time is on the learning – this is what training, in whatever form, is all about. Some people may disagree with this concentration on learning and feel that other, perhaps wider questions, should be posed. If this is what is required, a well-constructed reactionnaire can be used to supplement the questionnaire and asking for whatever reactions appear relevant. This approach will provide information, but the basic essential of *validation* and *evaluation* must remain the assessment of the *learning*.

THE CONSTRUCTION OF QUESTIONNAIRES

Although we are considering here the use of questionnaires at the end of a programme to assess the achievement of learning objectives during the programme, they can be used at any time during the programme, as suggested earlier. The same principles, for the validation of learning, apply at whatever stage they might be used – at the end of a session, a group of sessions, or at the end of a training day, and we have considered these approaches in a general way in Chapter 7. Figure 7.11 suggests one form of an acceptably effective, end of session reactionnaire, with its tick list supported by requirements placed on the learners to justify their scoring, etc.

There are, however (apart from the learning requirements), several aspects of questionnaires construction to be considered, some of which have already been mentioned when other instruments were being described.

THE SEMANTIC DIFFERENTIAL QUESTIONNAIRE (SDQ)

The majority of validation questionnaires fall within this description. The basic part of the questionnaire is a scoring bar or set of boxes between a set of opposites, the polarized descriptions, which are different semantically and usually take the form of antonyms. An example of the simplest SDQ is:

How hard did you work today?

Very hard _____ Not at all

This simple use of two polarized statements is not sufficiently sensitive to shades of meaning, and usually the score bar is divided into sections. These sections can be formed by vertical bars, by boxes or by symbols:

Very hard |__|__|__|__|__|__|__|__|__| Not at all

Very hard ☐ ☐ ☐ ☐ ☐ ☐ ☐ ☐ ☐ Not at all

Very hard   9 8 7 6 5 4 3 2 1 Not at all

In the first two examples, the learners are asked to place a tick or a cross in the space or box, the position of which most closely represents their views. In the numbered example, circles can be placed around the relevant number or a stroke placed through it. There seems to be little practical difference between the methods, but the requirement must be made clear to the people completing the questionnaire. Even so, it is quite common for completers to place a tick where they should be using a cross, and so on – this does not detract from the responses, except that it should make you think 'Did I make the scoring instruction sufficiently clear?'

Score identification

In some scoring bars with spaces or boxes, the bars are left as shown in the examples above; in others, numbers are placed above them to identify the discrete position of the scoring tick. In this way the tick position on each scoring bar used can be used arithmetically to analyse the completion of the questionnaire. There seems to be little comparative value weighting for any of the methods.

Some questionnaire designers argue that the use of numbers gives the incorrect impression that the analysis is a highly mathematically valid calculation, whereas this is not the case in such a subjective and arbitrary area.

Apart from their use in (albeit quasi-mathematical) analyses, the numbers can be helpful to the completers in identifying a place on each scale and its distance away from a pole.

Scale anchors

Each end of the scoring scale is anchored by a word or short phrase, antonyms being used to provide the semantic differential: the necessity to use suitable words has already been mentioned (see pages 126–29), but other anchor factors can determine the value of the scale. A consistent approach to placing the anchors has also been discussed – to avoid confusion and/or unconsidered completion of the scales, the 'good/very' and 'bad/not at all' anchors should be placed in the same position for all the scales in use. The general trend is for the better ratings to be placed on the left side of the scale, but there seems to be little problem if this placing is reversed – consistently.

Number of scale scoring positions

This is probably the most discussed, unresolved aspect of questionnaire construction. Two questions are raised:

1. Should there be an even or odd number of score positions?
2. How many score positions should be offered?

The principal argument against an odd number of rating positions is that there will always be a mid-number that will be viewed by many completers as the 'average' scoring. In most cases, average is not part of the possible scoring – the middle score is in effect avoiding the issue, 'sitting on the fence'. The supporters of the odd-numbered scale suggest that ample instruction in its completion should be given to the learners, to encourage them to think more deeply about the score they are giving and use the mid-position only if that score is the appropriate one. My personal preference is to avoid the possibility of averaging and use an even-numbered scale.

The other question requires much more consideration, and I am not aware of any research showing a 'correct' answer. Questionnaire constructors can be torn between minimum questionnaire entries and simple scorings on the basis that there will be a greater chance of the learners completing it effectively and not looking at what they might see as an over-imposing document. On the other hand, a simpler scoring scale in particular will not allow people to define their views as accurately as they might wish.

At the simplest, the rating scale can contain but two scoring possibilities – '1' or '2' – corresponding to the Yes/No of the knowledge tests, or the Agree/Disagree of the Thurstone Scale. Many people find this too restricting, particularly in the subjective areas of assessment where the fact is not black or white, but a shade of grey in between. How many shades you feel can be identified without too much trouble will determine the number of rating points above two. If you wish to use the smallest number of points, before settling for three remember the argument described above in which too many people might go for the neutral/average/don't know middle score rather than commit themselves. Too long a scale can confuse the completer who might be tempted, because of doubts about the fine details, to place the scoring marks in a haphazard way, concentrating about the central areas. The three-test described in the previous chapter had a ten-point scale, but this version is used in a particular situation and normally ten points might be too much to ask the completers to use in defining their views.

Where there may be a wide range of doubt or difficulty in definition, it is advisable to have a more extended scale than when the issues are very clear. In the latter case, perhaps a four-point scale might be sufficient, but in most cases in my experience a six-point scale gives sufficient latitude without being confusing. However, eight points would also seem to be acceptable.

Whether you use an odd- or even-numbered scale, and however you introduce it, you will always find that people will tend to place their ratings around the central area – the mid-number in odd-number scales, ratings 4 and 3 in a six-point scale. Perhaps this can be taken as a reflection of the validity of the training – it may have been too neutral or confusing to enable people to take a positive stance or, in human relations programmes, the intended enhanced interactive atmosphere was not achieved. If the scores do hover around the central area in too many cases, this will be a signal to start asking more probing questions about validity. There is always the possibility, of course, that the questions you are asking are not appropriate or are confusing themselves!

QUESTIONS TO ASK

Considerations similar to those applying to reactionnaires apply to validation questionnaires, but in this case selection is simple. Any questions posed in a validation questionnaire must relate to the purpose of validation, namely the assessment of achievement of the training programme's objective and methods, and the satisfaction of the learners' objectives. That is to say the extent of the *learning*. Consequently the questions will be directly concerned with learning:

- How much have you learned?
- What have you learned?
- If you haven't learned in all aspects, why not?

Answers to these questions should normally be sufficient to validate the learning. Some of this information – the extent of learning – will be obtained from a scoring scale:

During the programme, how much have you learned?

A lot   6   5   4   3   2   1   A little

It may also be necessary, particularly in programmes where earlier assessments have shown a wide variety of knowledge and skill within the learning group, to ask:

During the programme, how much have you had usefully confirmed?

A lot   6   5   4   3   2   1   A little

JUSTIFICATION

As suggested above, the two questions posed should give you sufficient information about the extent of learning, but the scales do not tell you more than this. Full validation will require information on what has been learned; what is going to be done with that learning; or why learning hasn't occurred. In other words, the completers of the validation questionnaires should be asked to justify their ratings, both good and bad.

This is achieved by adding, after the rating scale, questions that seek responses to the questions stated above. The learners can be asked, if they have given a 'good' rating to learning, to state what they have learned, and also what they are going to do with that learning. If they have given a 'bad' rating, they should be asked for the reasons why – responses might cover a wide spectrum of reasons, ranging from the environment to the trainer, similar to a reactionnaire, but related directly to and raised by the question of learning, or rather the lack of it.

Depending on the complexity of the training programme, the questions might relate to the total programme, in the case of short or subject-discrete courses, or to blocks of subjects. Recently I was involved in a training programme for trainers and managers that included the related but separate subjects of training needs analysis and evaluation. Consequently it was sensible to extend the end of programme questionnaire and divide it into two parts, one asking about TNA learning, the other about evaluation learning. On another occasion I was involved in a programme that included general communication, presentation skills and writing skills as three separate, but interrelated subjects. In this case, three sections asked the questions about the three main subjects, and a fourth section asked questions about the programme overall.

Figure 9.1 demonstrates one recommended form of end of programme validation questionnaire, with both learning questions and confirmation of previous learning questions, and a supporting, additional reactionnaire.

END OF PROGRAMME VALIDATION QUESTIONNAIRE

Please consider the learning programme that you have attended and complete the following, being completely honest in your assessments and answering the questions as fully as possible.

PART ONE: LEARNING

To what extent do you feel you have learned from the programme? (Please ring the score number that you feel most closely represents your views.)

Learned a lot   6   5   4   3   2   1   Learned nothing

If you have rated 6, 5 or 4, please describe a) what you have learned and b) what you intend to do with this learning on your return to work.

If you have rated 3, 2 or 1, please state as fully as possible the reasons why you gave this rating.

PART TWO: CONFIRMATION OF LEARNING

To what extent do you feel you have had previous learning (perhaps some you have forgotten) confirmed in a useful manner?

Confirmed a lot   6   5   4   3   2   1   Confirmed little

If you have rated 6, 5 or 4, please describe a) what has been confirmed and b) what you intend to do with this learning on your return to work.

If you have rated 3, 2 or 1, please state as fully as possible the reasons why you gave this rating.

PART THREE: ADDITIONAL INFORMATION (Alternative 1)

For every item place an 'X' in the scoring box that most closely represents how you feel about the programme. Also, please comment briefly on each item about your reasons for giving this score, particularly if your ratings are 3, 2 or 1.

	6	5	4	3	2	1	
Stimulating	□	□	□	□	□	□	Boring

Please comment briefly why you have given this rating

| Useful for my work | □ | □ | □ | □ | □ | □ | Useless |

Please comment briefly why you have given this rating

| Relevant to my work | □ | □ | □ | □ | □ | □ | Irrelevant |

Please comment briefly why you have given this rating

| Good discussions | □ | □ | □ | □ | □ | □ | Limited discussions |

Please comment briefly why you have given this rating

| Flexible structure | □ | □ | □ | □ | □ | □ | Rigid structure |

Please comment briefly why you have given this rating

| Well conducted | □ | □ | □ | □ | □ | □ | Poorly conducted |

Please comment briefly why you have given this rating

| Demanding | □ | □ | □ | □ | □ | □ | Undemanding |

Please comment briefly why you have given this rating

| Challenging | □ | □ | □ | □ | □ | □ | Patronizing |

Please comment briefly why you have given this rating

| Well spaced out | □ | □ | □ | □ | □ | □ | Too condensed |

Please comment briefly why you have given this rating

| Good use of time | □ | □ | □ | □ | □ | □ | Poor use of time |

Please comment briefly why you have given this rating

| Good level of activity | □ | □ | □ | □ | □ | □ | Poor level of activity |

Please comment briefly why you have given this rating

| My objectives achieved | □ | □ | □ | □ | □ | □ | My objectives not achieved |

Please comment briefly why you have given this rating

I would recommend the programme to my colleagues   YES □ NO □

Any other comments:

PART THREE: ADDITIONAL INFORMATION (Alternative 2)

1. Which parts of the event did you find the most useful?
2. Which parts of the event did you find the least useful?
3. Are there any parts you would have omitted? If so, which parts and why?
4. Is there anything you would have liked to have seen added to the event? What should have been removed to make room for it?
5. Which of your personal objectives were satisfied?
6. Which of your personal objectives were not satisfied?
7. Have you any other comments you wish to make?

Name .... Date ....

Figure 9.1 *End of programme validation questionnaire*

It is often useful to have the supplementary reactionnaire at the following times:

- the end of the first course of a new series;
- the mid-point in an extended programme;
- when an existing programme appears to be in some form of trouble.

The questions can be as suggested, or more specifically appropriate ones if there is programme remedial action to be considered. Alternative formats are suggested.

Figure 9.2 shows a recommended form of end of session, end of day or end of block of sessions validation questionnaire.

WHAT ABOUT THE TRAINER?

So far I have avoided any comments on the direct assessment of the trainer or facilitator by the learners. If anything, this is even more difficult to do in an objective way than evaluation of a programme. There is also the moral issue of whether learners should assess their trainers. Substantial arguments exist on both sides, as listed below.

For trainer assessment

- If the learners do not make any comments, who else is in a position to do so? Alternatives might be co-trainers (if there are any) or an observing training manager (who may only be able to do this on one occasion).

END OF SESSION, END OF DAY OR END OF BLOCK
OF SESSIONS VALIDATION

Please ring the scoring number which you feel is most
relevant for you.

1.   SESSION: USE OF PRACTICAL ACTIVITIES

Learned   6   5   4   3   2   1   Learned
a lot   nothing

If you have scored either 6, 5 or 4, please state briefly
what you have learned and how you intend to use it at
work.

If you have scored either 3, 2 or 1, please state as fully
as possible why you have given this score.

2.   SESSION: EFFECTIVE USE OF VIDEOS IN TRAINING

Learned   6   5   4   3   2   1   Learned
a lot   nothing

If you have scored either 6, 5 or 4, please state briefly
what you have learned and how you intend to use it at
work.

If you have scored either 3, 2 or 1, please state as fully
as possible why you have given this score.

Any other comments

Name .... Date ....

Figure 9.2   *End of session, end of day or end of block of sessions*
validation questionnaire

- The learners are on the receiving end of the trainer's approaches and are the only ones who can say how they reacted.
- Good material can be affected adversely by a poor trainer and the *training programme* may receive a bad assessment incorrectly.
- Organizations may be interested in the observed performance of their trainers or consultants and may seek a number of ways to obtain this information.

Against trainer assessment

- If the trainers know that they are to be assessed, with the results being made public, they may behave differently with the learners, the training taking a second place to the public image.
- The feelings of the learners can be biased for or against the trainer in many ways and for many reasons, which they may not identify themselves.
- The learners are unlikely to be professionally qualified to comment on the trainers' skill and their views may be inappropriate if they do not understand the techniques used to help them to learn.
- The trainers' assessments may be skewed according to whether the learners liked or didn't like them; accepted or rejected any necessarily hard training; preferred/enjoyed their out-of-class socializing or non-socializing etc.
- Individual or sub-group views may be biased if they felt that the trainers either supported their views or disagreed with them.
- Often, a more effective assessment of the trainers' skills etc can be made from the validation of the training programme – were the training objectives and those of the learners met? If so, there can be little wrong with the trainers' methods and approaches. (There is, however, a parallel with the statement made earlier that good material can be wasted by a poor trainer: poor material, although it will never replace good material, can be improved by a skilled trainer, with the resulting better assessment of the training.)

If it is decided that a trainer assessment should be introduced, as with training overall it will be necessary to design the format, bearing in mind that any results are unlikely to be objective analyses but, rather, subjective reactions. It is essential that the same disciplines should be applied to their design as we considered in the construction of validation questionnaires. Tick lists alone, without space for justification of a scoring, should be avoided, since the discipline of commenting in this way will tend to make the learners consider and report more objectively. Remember that, if the programme contains more than one trainer, separate assessment sheets will be required for each trainer, or the single sheet should identify clearly the trainer on whom the assessment is being made.

A possible assessment sheet for general assessment of a trainer is included here as Figure 9.3.

TRAINER ASSESSMENT

Please answer the following questions about ....
(one of) the trainer(s) on this course. Please try to be as honest and positively critical as possible as your responses will help the trainer in his/her personal development. In addition to rating each question by ringing the relevant number, comment as fully as possible to justify your ratings.

How well did the trainer:	Very well					Poorly
Interact with the learning group? Why?	6	5	4	3	2	1
Use the most effective techniques to help you learn? How?	6	5	4	3	2	1
Show knowledge of the subjects involved? How?	6	5	4	3	2	1
Help you learn? How?	6	5	4	3	2	1
Vary the content of the programme? How?	6	5	4	3	2	1
Use the time available? How?	6	5	4	3	2	1
Use presentational skills? How?	6	5	4	3	2	1
Use presentational aids? Which ones and how?	6	5	4	3	2	1
Overall rating Why?	6	5	4	3	2	1
Any other comments						

Figure 9.3 *Trainer assessment questionnaire*

Replacement or additional questions can be used and, in circumstances other than a straightforward training course, it will be necessary to modify the questions accordingly.

ACTION PLANNING

Although action planning is not a direct form of validation or assessment, it is such a powerful tool, with a wide range of uses, that it must be considered an essential part of evaluation. In fact, if no other evaluation tool can be used, the action plan *must* be used, hopefully with the opportunity for follow up at a later date. Consequently, I would recommend that *every* training and learning programme close with an action plan.

The action plan is a commitment by the learners to implement, when they return to work, the learning they have achieved and identified in the end of programme validation. If the latter is not used, the action plan entries make a validation implication themselves. Items included in the plan will be learning points taken from the programme, and as a result it can be seen whether the intended objectives of the programme have been understood and accepted. Variation between the action plans of the learners is natural, but some variations, by their inclusion or exclusion, may indicate particularly good or particularly bad aspects of the programme.

The essential links between training and work have been stressed throughout this book, and the action plan is one of the most effective instruments for strengthening these links. The simple act of planning action based on the learning immediately relates the learners to their working environment. If the action plan is taken away and used – by the learner in the implementation of the learning, and by their managers in performing longer-term evaluation and control of implementation – no forced or artificial links are necessary; it becomes part of the work $\Rightarrow$ training/learning $\Rightarrow$ work integrated cycle.

An action plan format

The format of an action plan should be:

- simple and straightforward;
- clear and unambiguous;
- that it contains items that can be implemented by the learner, with or without other resources;

- owned by the learner;
- that it contains specific information that is time-bounded for implementation.

If the plan is a simple, clear document, there will be less learner resistance to its completion and implementation than if it is a complex, overdemanding document. The learner must have a substantial say in its format, and complete control over the items included – this ensures that the plan is owned by the learner, with a significant likelihood of its implementation.

Figure 9.4 suggests a simple format for the action plan, leading the learners in only three headings and leaving them to decide on the detail and amount of planning.

PERSONAL ACTION PLAN

ACTION PLAN ITEMS	HOW TO IMPLEMENT	WHEN, BY WHEN
1.		
2.		
3.		
4.		

Figure 9.4 *Action plan format*

The number of action items should not be too great – three or four is a reasonable number – and in the 'How to . . .' column the learner should consider materials, resources, etc that might be needed in the implementation. The plans should always be time-bounded with a starting/finishing commitment.

Producing the action plan

1. Precede the completion of the action plan with the justified end of programme validation questionnaire, in which the learners identify and reflect on what they have learned and what they wish to do with this learning. (If a Learning Log has been used, this will also prove useful in reminding them of lessons learned.)

2. Give ample time for the learners then to consider:
   - their personal action objectives;
   - priorities among these objectives.
3. Have the learners complete their action plans, taking special note of:
   - the implementability of their plans;
   - what materials and other resources (including people) they might need;
   - the time factors involved;
   - strategies and tactics for implementing the plans;
   - the effect of their plans on others;
   - any possible obstacles to implementation;
   - any special factors that will help their implementation.
4. It is a useful discipline, once the learners have identified their planned items, for them to consider prioritization, rather than either taking them as they thought of them, or implementing first the least important (often the simplest) items.
5. Let the learners pair off so that they can have one-to-one discussions with a partner of their choice. This enables obstacles, additional resources, alternative methods of implementation and more effective strategies to be raised.
6. Have the learners commit themselves to implementation and discussing it with their line manager immediately on their return to work (hopefully a post-programme debriefing session has been arranged).
7. Agree, as far as is possible without the presence of the line manager, how the implementation will be monitored and by whom.

In addition, the trainer might usefully keep a copy of the action plan, with the learners' agreement, to help in the medium- and longer-term evaluation processes.

There are several approaches to processing the action plan, principal among which are:

- The learner completes a personal action plan and takes this away from the programme to implement, with or without the intervention of the line manager.
- A copy is made for the trainer to retain for possible involvement in the medium- or longer-term evaluation process.
- The trainer sends a letter to the learner, with the agreement of the line manager, seeking information on the implementation or otherwise of the action plan.
- The learners compose the above letter and include a copy of the action plan.

Whichever approach is taken will depend to a large extent on the form that has been agreed for the medium- and longer-term evaluation processes, of which the learners and the trainer should be aware.

NOW OR LATER?

The final and frequently discussed aspect of end of programme validation concerns whether the validation reactionnaire/questionnaire should be completed by the learners during the event or delayed until they have returned to work.

The principal arguments for *during* the event include:

- the event and its contents are fresh in their mind and they will be able to comment readily;
- there will be certain parts of their learning standing out above others, and these obviously important aspects will be the ones on which they comment;
- there is the opportunity for the learning group to discuss their views with each other;
- the trainer is given immediate feedback;
- unclear statements can be clarified immediately;
- questions raised can be cleared or promised an early response by the trainer;
- (apart from any participants who had to leave early) 100 per cent response is guaranteed.

The principal arguments against *during* the event include:

- the participants may be in a state of euphoria because of an exciting event;
- the participants may be in a state of depression because of an unsuccessful event;
- the trainer was a very well-liked personality;
- the trainer was not liked or respected;
- going home is uppermost in their minds;
- there is an anti-questionnaire feeling;
- dominant members exert an influence on the views of others;
- some people prefer to delay their views until they have had a longer period to reflect/until they can relate the learning to their work.

There are equally arguments for and against delaying the completion of the validation until the learners have returned to work, perhaps a delay period of two or three weeks.

The arguments for *delaying* completion include:

- the learners are given time to consider the value of the event and their learning;
- the learners are given time to assess the realism of the implementation of their learning and their action plans;
- the debriefing meeting has taken place with their line managers and further thoughts have emerged from this discussion;
- completion takes place away from the artificial/euphoric/antipathetic atmosphere of the training event;
- no embarrassment is felt if adverse personal comments are made, with the relevant person not present.

Arguments against *delaying* completion can include:

- return cannot be guaranteed without a foolproof method (in the case of small numbers possibly the major argument, as the non-returns might contain the most important comments – positive or negative);
- return to work and outstanding tasks to be done take priority and completion is forgotten;
- completion is simply forgotten;
- there is no intention to complete the questionnaire;
- the learner does not wish to commit adverse comments to paper;
- the event and its content have slipped into the mists of time and memory;
- there is a reduced/reducing commitment to support the trainers with feedback.

Support for a delayed return

If it has been decided that the validation reactionnaire and/or questionnaire should be given to the learners for return following a period of time back at work, techniques can be employed to ensure (as far as is possible) return of the data. These can include the following:

- Arrange with the relevant line managers (or some other responsible personnel away from the training function) that they should ensure return as agreed with the learners.

- Follow up by telephone or in writing (preferably the former) directly with the non-responding learner(s), stressing the importance and value of the validation instrument.
- Give the learners a stamped, trainer-addressed envelope with the blank questionnaire – clip this envelope securely to the questionnaire.
- Send the questionnaire/reactionnaire to the learners at their place of work at an agreed period following the training event – this might be routed through the line managers, so reinforcing the importance of the questionnaire and supporting the 'encouragement' by the line manager for the learner to respond. The completed response could be returned via the line manager.

A compromise approach can be adopted, particularly if time is restricted towards the end of the event, by having the learners complete a short questionnaire/reactionnaire that seeks the most important, immediate feedback information. A longer enquiry can then be sent to the learners about a week later. One question that can be included in this second enquiry might ask whether their first reactions have changed since they have had time to reflect.

An alternative to the traditional questionnaire issue might be, if the learners or some of them have the facilities, to send the enquiry by computer network or through the Internet/e-mail or similar.

10

Evaluation of Open and Distance Learning Programmes

In most respects the evaluation of self-instruction (or open/distance learning or programmed instruction as the packages are sometimes called) is very similar to that for direct training course types of programmes. The principal difference is that for most, if not all the time that the learner is following the programme, there is no contact between them and a trainer – or at least usually not face to face. However, the use of self-instruction programmes is not the simplistic issue of sending the package to the learner, who is then expected to work through it and learn – although many users see it thus and also see it as an alternative to the use of any other resource whatsoever. Few people can learn from a self-instruction package in isolation.

The packages or programmes are described under a number of names, the commonest being:

- open learning;
- distance learning;
- self-instruction programmes;
- programmed learning or text;
- correspondence courses – the forerunner of the present approaches.

In general I shall use the title 'open learning' in this chapter.

There are some differences in fact between these programmes other than the names, but the basic approach of all is that the learner, at the workplace or at home, works through an instructional package alone. The material in the package will usually be self-instructional text, which follows a pattern of information – question – answer – review. This text can be supplemented by videos, interactive videos, computer programs, interactive CDs and/or many other forms of support.

The packages are obtained by the learner either from a central resources centre/a resource library or purchased from a commercial organization. The first case often – though unfortunately not always – includes the provision of professional support via the telephone or electronic mail. Otherwise, the learner is left with the package, which hopefully is sufficiently well constructed to avoid problems.

Open learning packages are now obtainable for a very wide range of subjects, but unfortunately some of these do not lend themselves easily to the medium, particularly if the package is unsupported. Open learning is essentially the transfer of knowledge to practical skill by in-package activities and exercises, followed by workplace implementation. The approach obviously lends itself easily to operations and procedures, less easily to the more general types of skills and, with no live support, not at all to behavioural and human resource skills.

THE EFFECTIVE USE OF OPEN LEARNING PACKAGES

The recommended stages for a learner using an open learning package will include:

1. Agreement with the learner's line manager that training in the subject is necessary.
2. Agreement with the learner's line manager that the learning will best be approached by means of open learning.
3. Agreement with the line manager that sufficient time to learn from the package is made available during working hours and all necessary facilities will be available.
4. The line manager or learner obtains the relevant open learning package from an appropriate source (let us assume here that this is the central resource centre within the organization staffed by training professionals and/or open learning experts).
5. The learner commences working through the open learning package.
6. If problems arise during use of the package, these can be resolved by discussion with the line manager, another local expert, or contact with the central resource.
7. During use of the package, the learner will be performing exercises and activities supporting the text.
8. Following completion of the package, agreement will be reached with the line manager for opportunities to be made available for the learner to implement the learning.

EVALUATION OF OPEN LEARNING

The first aspect of the evaluation of open learning is the decision, before use of any package starts, about whether the selected package, albeit appropriate to satisfy the training need, is of a satisfactory quality (see Figure 10.1). This is of considerable importance in written open learning packages, perhaps more so than in the case of direct training courses.

Evaluating the quality of written open learning materials

Consider whether the content of the written material:

Is in line with the values and culture of the organization employing the learner

Is in line with the approaches, techniques, models, etc acceptable within the learner's employing organization

Is written to take account, as far as possible, of the different learning styles of potential users

Strikes a good balance between complexity and simplicity, difficulty and ease

Contains relevant information only

Provides a good balance between textual information, exercises, activities, other reading, case studies and, where relevant, supporting video and computer material

Provides, where necessary, appropriate and relevant computer and video programs.

Figure 10.1 *Evaluating the quality of written open learning materials*

The subsequent evaluation of open learning will follow the normal processes of evaluation of training and learning and also the cycle of stages described above. A typical approach will be as follows:

1. There can be discussion between the learner, the line manager and trainer about the comparative values of different approaches to learning, including open learning, for the particular learner in this specific situation. A number of issues, additional to the appropriateness aspect, can be involved here – availability of other methods, the learning style of the learner, immediacy of the need, cost, need for the learner not to be away from the workplace (although the time for open learning must be sacrosanct).
2. Following agreement on the use of open learning, the provision by the resource centre of the appropriate package is arranged.

These first two steps, although not apparently concerned with evaluation, in fact set the scene for the start of the evaluation process, with the involvement of the trainer ensuring that the appropriate steps are being taken and open learning is the most effective, cost- and value-effective way to satisfy the learning need.

3. It is essential that, before the package is commenced, the line manager and the learner should meet for a pre-programme briefing in exactly the same way as recommended for other forms of training.
4. An essential inclusion is an initial test covering the material in the package. If this is not included, and the package is supplied by the resource centre of the organization, those professionals should enable the learner to perform an appropriate test before starting work on the package.
5. Another essential part of the package, again provided by the resource centre if it is not an integral part of the package, are interim activities and exercises and interim tests of learning. These might be monitored by the centre, so supporting the learner by providing an external source of evaluation of both the package and of the learner's learning progress.
6. In the same way that an action plan is completed at the end of a direct training course, so should there be one at the end of the learning package, again to ensure that the learners commit themselves to action as a result of the training.

7. The package should include a final test of learning, but there is much to commend a final validation being administered by the external source. This can give valuable information about both the package and the learner – to the learner, the trainer and the line manager. It correlates with the normal end of programme validation questionnaire but, because of the different nature of the learning processes, can be quite different in format.

8. When the learner has completed the open learning package and the end of programme validation instrument(s), a debriefing meeting should be held between the learner and the line manager and, if necessary, the trainer. One element to be included in this debriefing is discussion about whether the learner needs any further training, perhaps of a different nature, to reinforce the essentially knowledge learning of the open learning package. This might be attendance on a short training course in which the opportunity for practice of the learned skills is given, before they are attempted in the workplace. It is also the opportunity for the learner and the line manager to discuss the implementation of the action plan and make arrangements for medium- and/or longer-term monitoring of progress.

9. Medium- and longer-term evaluation should take place (see the next chapter for a discussion of this) with the involvement of the learner and the line manager and/or the trainer.

As you will see, the process is little different from other forms of training and development, the principal differences being those carried out on completion of the package.

END OF OPEN LEARNING PACKAGE VALIDATION QUESTIONNAIRE

Two validation questionnaires would seem to be relevant in most cases, unless there is something included in the package itself. The first will be in the same format as the first part of Figure 9.1, the end of programme validation questionnaire. This is repeated, slightly modified, as Figure 10.2.

The other questionnaire is directed mainly at validation of the open learning programme itself and a format I have found useful is illustrated in Figure 10.3.

Please consider the learning programme that you have just completed and answer the following questions, being completely honest in your assessments and answering the questions as fully as possible.

PART ONE: LEARNING

To what extent do you feel you have learned from the programme? (Please ring the score number that you feel most closely represents your views.)

Learned a lot   6   5   4   3   2   1   Learned nothing

If you have rated 6, 5 or 4, please describe a) what you have learned and b) what you intend to do with this learning on your return to work.

If you have rated 3, 2 or 1, please state as fully as possible the reasons why you gave this rating.

PART TWO: CONFIRMATION OF LEARNING

To what extent do you feel you have had previous learning (perhaps some you have forgotten) confirmed in a useful manner?

Confirmed a lot   6   5   4   3   2   1   Confirmed little

If you have rated 6, 5 or 4, please describe a) what has been confirmed and b) what you intend to do with this learning on your return to work.

If you have rated 3, 2 or 1, please state as fully as possible the reasons why you gave this rating.

Figure 10.2 *End of open learning programme validation questionnaire*

EVALUATING MEDIA-BASED LEARNING METHODS

Media-based learning methods are the new technological techniques of the learning process, whether stand alone – for example, computer-based training – or as part of a training course or open learning programme. Their value and validity have to be assessed as for other forms of training, and in this are more like open learning than direct training course approaches. Before they are introduced to the learners,

Where scoring scales are provided, please ring the score rating you wish to give and also please comment as fully as you can.

1. As a result of the learning package, were you able to meet
   (a) your learning objectives?

   Completely   6   5   4   3   2   1   Not at all

   If you have rated 1 to 3, please comment why you have given this score.

   (b) the programme's stated objectives?

   Completely   6   5   4   3   2   1   Not at all

   If you have rated 1 to 3, please comment why you have given this score.

2. Which activities helped you learn the most?

3. Which activities were less helpful? The least helpful? Why?

4. Did you find any instructions difficult to follow? If so, which ones?

5. Were any of the activities uninteresting? Which ones? Why?

6. Were you given sufficient information to enable you to perform the activities?

   Sufficient   6   5   4   3   2   1   Insufficient

   If rating is 3, 2 or 1, please state in what way.

7. Were there any instances in which you felt you were given too much information? Which ones and to what extent too much?

8. Were the instructions and the material always clear and understandable?

   Always   6   5   4   3   2   1   Never

   If not, which parts were not?

9. How much time did you spend on the programme?

10. Was the time you had available sufficient to enable you to complete the programme as you would have wished?

Sufficient   6   5   4   3   2   1   Insufficient

11. How accessible was a trainer/tutor/other person to provide help?

Very   6   5   4   3   2   1   Not at all

If you have scored 4, 3, 2 or 1, to what limited extent?

12. Was the person mentioned in (11) helpful when asked for assistance?

Very   6   5   4   3   2   1   Not at all

If you have scored 4, 3, 2, or 1, to what limited extent?

13. How often did you have to ask for assistance?

14. How isolated did you feel completing the package?

Very   6   5   4   3   2   1   Not at all

15. How difficult did you find the package as a whole?

Very   6   5   4   3   2   1   Not at all

16. Any other comments?

Figure 10.3 *Open learning validation questionnaire*

a number of critical questions must be answered positively. Figure 10.4 suggests some of these questions.

Also required is an end of programme validation questionnaire in the same format as Figure 10.3, with some of the questions modified and others relating directly to the type of training added. For example, questions relating to the use of the technological equipment, its availability, ease of use etc might need to be asked.

EVALUATING THE QUALITY OF MEDIA-BASED LEARNING METHODS

Does the learning area, wherever this might be, have the necessary technological equipment and back-up services?

Will any additional technological provision have to be made to enable the learners to complete the open learning programme?

Do the learners (when completing an open learning programme with media-based learning methods) have the necessary skills in operating the hardware and software?

Does the learning material give clear, sufficient/comprehensive, logical instructions on the use of the equipment:

■ as equipment?
■ for the learning programme purposes?

What is the minimum operating knowledge necessary?

To what extent is a trainer's presence required?

Figure 10.4 *Evaluating the quality of media-based learning methods*

In the evaluation of open learning, with or without multi-media technology involvement, you will see that, apart from the differences introduced by the medium, the approaches are very similar to evaluation of direct training. Although the questions may be different, it is essential not to rely on tick lists alone, questions should also be posed to enable the learners to justify their ratings. The more the learner is required to write (within acceptable bounds), the more they are likely to reflect on and consider their learning.

11

Post-programme Evaluation

Too often evaluation (or what passes for it) does not extend beyond the end of programme validation, but then all that has been assessed is the satisfaction of the training programme objectives and the immediate objectives of the learners. This goes some way if it has been performed effectively, but it is not complete evaluation and certainly does not lead to an assessment of the value effectiveness of the learning.

In order to do this, three further stages are necessary:

> 1. **Post-programme debriefing**
> 2. **Medium-term evaluation**
> 3. **Longer-term evaluation**

Stages 2 and 3 can be combined as required.

POST-PROGRAMME DEBRIEFING

This subject was raised in Chapter 3 along with the description of the pre-programme briefing session. It should take place as soon as possible after the training programme, preferably during the next few days and certainly within a week. The learners and their line managers should meet, as arranged at the pre-programme briefing meeting. This meeting is as important, if not more so, than the first, having as one of its main objectives the commitment and agreement of the line managers to support the learners' action plans. The objectives include:

- demonstrating active interest in the learner's training and career progress;
- demonstrating active interest in the learner's action plan;

- discussing and agreeing the learner's action plan with the learner;
- confirming support and resources for the implementation of the action plan;
- agreeing the implementation of the action plan;
- agreeing interim support and final review meetings.

It should go without saying that this commitment should be sincere and followed through as agreed. Part of the line manager's support is their personal involvement where necessary and obtaining the support, commitment and services of other staff.

Guidelines for the performance of the post-programme debriefing interview were discussed in Chapter 3 and summarized in Figure 3.4.

Line managers should be in contact with the training programme trainers, contact that usually happens only when something has gone wrong. Feedback from the learner should certainly be passed on to the appropriate trainers and, if appropriate, a trainer who was involved with the programme might be invited to sit in on the meeting. This should be *in support* of the line managers, not to supplant them, such as when there are problems of implementing the learning or where questions might arise about further training and development. But the principal reason for the meeting is discussion about the implementation of the learner's action plan.

MEDIUM- AND LONGER-TERM EVALUATION

Neither training nor learning stop at the end of the programme and with the production of a sophisticated action plan. Training and learning are all about change, and change is the practical demonstration of these in the workplace so that the operation of the task, job or role can be improved. Ensuring that these changes take place is the responsibility of the learners and their line managers, a responsibility that must be monitored and reviewed to bring to a close the process of evaluation.

The best-planned and designed training will never be anything more than an expensive, interesting exercise if what has been learned is not put into action in the work environment. Training for training's sake is a futile exercise and, in the world of work, the amassing of knowledge is costly and worthless if that knowledge is not put to practical use. On the other side of the coin, we still hear of learners returning to work full of enthusiasm to put their learning into practice, only to be told

'You can forget all that; this is how we do it here!' However, if all the partners in the training quintet are playing their parts, particularly the line managers in whose hands the support for implementation lies, there should be no problems other than practical ones.

Realistically the trainer's role ends with the completion of the programme and the departure of the learners with their action plans. The principal responsibility for post-programme implementation lies with the line manager, who selected the training, paid for it and will expect a return on the investment. But, naturally, trainers will retain an interest in the results of their labours long after the event, even if they have no practical part to play in a follow up. However, they should have a more active part as members of the quintet, strengthening the links by more continuous involvement. But the final responsibility *must* lie with the line manager, the trainers being involved by invitation, at their own request, if necessary.

The final stages in the evaluation process are assessments of the extent to which the training has been implemented effectively and has had a positive effect on the work of the organization, the learners growing in stature as a result. The immediate post-programme action is putting into practice the items of the action plan (as a minimum objective), preferably with the active and continuing support of the line manager. Subsequent to this, assessments can be made after an interval of, say, three months – the medium-term evaluation – and then/or at a longer interval of 12 months – the longer-term evaluation. Ideally, arrangements for these subsequent evaluations should be made at the post-programme debriefing meeting.

Medium/longer term evaluation methods

There are several ways in which these evaluations can be made:

- line manager observation and assessment of the performed activities;
- trainer observation and assessment of the performed activities;
- follow-up questionnaire sent to both the learners and their line manager;
- structured interview conducted by the line manager or trainer;
- telephone follow-up interview by the trainer;
- critical incident analysis;
- Learning Logs;
- repertory grid.

LINE MANAGER OR TRAINER OBSERVATION AND ASSESSMENT OF THE PERFORMED ACTIVITIES

Observation of the learner trying to put the learning into action at work must be the most effective method of evaluating the learning and confirming that it is being used as it was intended. The starting point of this observation, by whoever performs it, will be the original task analysis, which will have detailed the operations and other requirements of the learned task or role. The benefit of having such an analysis in a permanent, written form is that it ensures that nothing is missed and subjective values are kept to a minimum. The observation technique will depend on the nature of the aspect to be observed, whether it is an operational task, a behavioural role, or a mixture of both. Activity and behaviour analysis instruments such as those described in Chapter 7 can be used, being constructed from the task analysis base.

It should be relatively simple for the line manager to make such observations within the routine of daily work, perhaps making some special efforts to observe particular, possibly infrequent, elements of the task. The line manager might keep a record, including checklists, of observations made and to be made, so introducing a discipline that ensures that the practice is carried out. Otherwise it is too easy to allow the follow up to fail by default.

Problems can arise, not only if some aspects are carried out infrequently, but also if the task or role is extended and requires further or continuous observation. In such cases it may be that, with the best will in the world, the manager cannot afford the time to carry out the observation or, as happens sometimes, the line manager is not always in a practical position to observe the learner. The training organization might then provide someone to carry out the observations in lieu of the manager. Obviously this is a more expensive approach in terms of time and money, especially if the task is an extended or complex one. The trainer-observers must be fully aware of the job environment and all aspects of its content. The checklists referred to above are essential parts of the observer's toolkit and, particularly with extended tasks, a suitable schedule must be formed to ensure observation of all elements in the most effective manner possible.

Perhaps the strongest argument against using the trainer, rather than the manager, is that the trainer will be seen as an observer whereas the manager becomes part of the scenery. This argument is not of course insurmountable, and time spent in setting the scene effectively can allay many of the natural concerns of the people observed. But this takes more time and expense.

One effective approach is *activity sampling*, in which the observer spreads the observing periods over time – hours, days, even weeks – ensuring that all aspects are seen and assessed. This again may introduce additional expense, certainly additional time, for the observer, and an extended period of observation can produce contaminatory effects. However, in some circumstances it may be the only possible approach.

THE FOLLOW-UP QUESTIONNAIRE

This method is probably the most frequently used of all the follow-up evaluation approaches. It is the simplest and also the least expensive, but it is not necessarily the most effective. There must be a foolproof method of ensuring that responses are made and the questionnaire must be planned to obtain responses that are as comprehensive and as objective as possible.

The follow-up questionnaire should use as its base the learners' action plans, since the principal objective is to determine to what extent the action plans have been implemented and with what effectiveness. The questionnaire can of course serve more than this basic, albeit essential, objective – post-programme consideration of the training course is a common secondary intent – but any others must not complicate the questionnaire to the extent that the major reason for its use is not fulfilled.

The construction of follow-up questionnaires

The objectives will include:

> - Confirmation of the learning achieved during the training programme
> - Action taken to implement the action plan
> - Assessment of the effectiveness of the learning implementation

The questions posed to achieve these objectives will require the learners to refer back to their action plans, and in so doing be reminded, if this is necessary, of what they contracted to do. These questions will include:

- Which items of the action plan have been implemented?
- What degree of success has been achieved from this?
- Which items have not (yet) been implemented?
- Why haven't they been implemented?
- Did any planned actions fail in implementation?
- What reasons emerged for their failure?
- What are the plans for further action:
    - on unsuccessful or non-implemented plans?
    - beyond this stage?

These are the essential areas for which the questionnaire should be designed, but depending on the situation you may wish to obtain more information at the same time, usually of a reaction nature. Perhaps you have newly instituted a scheme whereby the line managers are more involved in training and evaluation; consequently further questions might be added along these lines. Such questions could include ones seeking information about:

- The nature of the debriefing meeting and its outcomes.
- The support promised and received from the manager.
- The support arranged and received from colleagues.
- The extent of the value of post-programme support.

Figure 11.1 suggests a questionnaire in this format.

One of the arguments against the use of the end of programme validation questionnaire or reactionnaire in the final stages of the course itself is that the learners may not be in a position to give a full and reflected response. The medium-term evaluation can be an opportunity to seek more reflected views about the training if it is felt that the immediate ones were contaminated. However, it must be remembered that mixing the purpose of a questionnaire to too great an extent can have unfortunate results.

If you decide to extend the range of the approach, a questionnaire such as that shown in Figure 11.2 (Figure 9.1 modified) can be used.

MEDIUM-TERM EVALUATION ACTION QUESTIONNAIRE

Course attended .... Dates ....

PART ONE: When you completed the training programme, you con-tracted to implement an action plan which detailed the following items:

1.

2.

3.   etc

Would you please answer the following questions as completely as you can.

1.   Which items of your action plan have you implemented so far?
2.   What degree of success have you achieved in respect of these items?
3.   To what factors or reasons do you attribute your success in implementing these items?
4.   Which items of your action plan have you not yet implemented?
5.   Which of these items have you tried but failed to implement?
6.   Why did this occur?
7.   Which items have you not yet attempted to implement?
8.   Why have you not yet attempted these?
9.   What plans do you have to:
     – attempt to rectify your unsuccessful items?
     – implement the as yet unattempted items?
10. Have you any additional plans? Please comment.

PART TWO: It will help our organization of training and the involvement of different people if you could answer the following questions, the responses to which will be kept confidential.

Did you have a debriefing meeting with your manager on your return to work?
If so, how quickly after the course did this take place?
What was the nature of the debriefing meeting and its outcomes?
What was the extent of the support promised by your manager?
What was the extent of the support received from your manager?
What was the extent of any support arranged with colleagues?
What was the extent of any support received from colleagues?
How valuable do you feel was the post-programme support?
Any other comments you wish to make?

Figure 11.1   *Medium-term evaluation questionnaire*

QUESTIONNAIRE RELATING TO THE TRAINING PROGRAMME YOU ATTENDED

Course attended .... Dates ....

Now that some time has passed, please consider the learning programme that you attended and complete the following, being completely honest in your assessments and answering the questions as fully as possible.

LEARNING

To what extent do you feel you learned from the programme? (Please ring the score number that you feel most closely represents your views.)

Learned a lot   6   5   4   3   2   1   Learned nothing

If you have rated 6, 5 or 4, please describe what you learned.

If you have rated 3, 2 or 1, please state as fully as possible the reasons why you gave this rating.

Figure 11.2 *Medium-term evaluation learning questionnaire*

FOLLOW UP WITH THE LINE MANAGER

In this type of approach the trainer can try to involve the manager in the evaluation, either from an information point of view or through direct involvement. If the line managers are not to be directly involved it can be useful to inform them of the progress of the evaluation by sending the questionnaire through them. (It will almost certainly not be politic to require the completed sheets to be returned to you via them, however, as this might inhibit the responses of the learners.) Doing this you are at least keeping line managers aware of the evaluation progress and may even encourage them to seek ways of being more involved.

The other principal method of involving the line manager in this first stage post-programme evaluation is to send them a progress questionnaire. This would be sent at the same time as that sent to the learners, and with the learners' agreement would include a copy of the action plan. The aim is to help the line managers in their follow up of implementation progress, to involve them in the post-programme evaluation and encourage discussion with the learners. The questionnaire itself is a modification of the one sent to the learner and is shown as Figure 11.3.

Course reviewed .... Dates ....

PART ONE: When .... completed the training programme, they contracted to implement an action plan which detailed the following items:

1.

2.

3. etc

Would you please answer the following questions as completely as you can from your own knowledge or observation.

1. Which items of the action plan do you know that they have implemented so far?
2. What degree of success have they achieved in respect of these items?
3. To what factors or reasons do you attribute their success in implementing these items?
4. Which items of the action plan have not yet been implemented?
5. Which of these items have they tried but failed to implement?
6. Why did this occur?
7. Which items have they not yet attempted to implement?
8. Why have they not been attempted?
9. What plans have you discussed with the learner to:
    – attempt to rectify the unsuccessful items?
    – implement the as yet unattempted items?
10. Have you any other comments?

PART TWO: It will help our organization of training and the involvement of different people if you could answer the following questions.

Did you have a debriefing meeting with the learner on their return to work? If so, how quickly after the course did this take place?
What was the nature of the debriefing meeting and its outcomes?
What was the extent of the support you promised?
What has been the extent of the support you have given?
What was the extent of any support arranged with colleagues?
What was the extent of any support received from colleagues?
How valuable do you feel the post-programme interactions were?
Any other comments you wish to make?

Figure 11.3 *Medium-term evaluation questionnaire*
(line manager version)

The post-programme evaluation questionnaire/reactionnaire can be more varied even than the ones used at the end of the programme and it is easy to go beyond the bounds of evaluation, particularly when the organization demands answers to certain questions. But three points are all important:

1. What do I want to know that will form part of a realistic evaluation? (Normally this will relate directly to the action plan completed by the learner.)
2. What form of questionnaire will be the most effective?
3. How can I ensure a satisfactory (complete) rate of return?

My own experiences of using questionnaires with both learners and their line managers have been very varied, ranging from a total correlation of the replies (suggesting that they have a close working relationship), to responses that gave the impression that the manager was reporting on a different person. In these latter cases, after some investigation, it was found that the manager was either located away from the learner and rarely saw their work, or that there was little effective interaction – the manager was just not interested in the learner provided the work was completed efficiently. The signals evident in the responses usually give good clues when there is something amiss.

STRUCTURED FOLLOW-UP INTERVIEWS

This is the other main method of performing a medium-term evaluation, and both interviews and questionnaires have their supporters. The negative aspect of the interview with the learner is that it is usually more expensive than using a questionnaire. This cost increases considerably if the learners, although belonging to one organization, are located throughout the country or, even more so, internationally. Some of the costs can be avoided if the line manager, rather than a remote trainer, conducts the interview, but the position has to be weighed up carefully as the line manager may be too 'close' to the learner, or there may be other factors that prevent a complete result being obtained. The interview approach can be the same whoever conducts it, and there are advantages in ensuring this consistent approach in an organization through training and education.

The interview approach

The objectives, both primary and secondary, set for the follow-up questionnaire are reflected in those for the interview, and the learners' action plans again form the base for the approach. The important points listed for the use of interviews are very similar to those for questionnaires:

- What do I want to know that will form part of a realistic evaluation? (Normally this will relate directly to the action plan completed by the learner.)
- What form of interview will be the most effective?
- Is the interview approach the most (cost-)effective one?

The interview will consist of a discussion between the interviewer (frequently a trainer) and the learner (and, separately, the line manager). If the results are to be valid, the form of a number of interviews must be the same. In this way, in addition to obtaining information, valid comparisons can be made between the reactions of learners. Structuring will help this process considerably.

Interview structures

There is no set structure for follow-up interviews as this will depend on prevailing circumstances, but it is strongly recommended that a general structure should be followed to ensure consistency as far as possible. The same questions, and wherever possible the same words, should certainly be used for the follow up of a similar group. But the interviewer should avoid making the interview so tightly structured that other subjects are not allowed to enter the discussion or the interviewer misses valuable clues by concentrating on the narrow path.

The basic behaviour of the interviewer will be that of posing questions; some comments have been made earlier on the type of questions an interviewer asks, and there is considerable literature on interview techniques. The responses and other contributions of the learner can be recorded on paper, cassette recorder, or even on video, although the latter creates its own problems. Of the many types of questions, the following will normally be the most useful:

- Open questions
- Testing understanding questions
- Reflecting
- Closed questions (when their use is relevant)

Ones to avoid are:

- Closed questions (too frequent and when this form is not appropriate)
- Leading questions
- Multiple or ambiguous questions
- Rhetorical questions

Apart from advice about the questions to ask, the other major guidance must be *Listen more than you talk, but listen effectively,* because you are seeking information from the learner.

Interview format

Although, as stated earlier, many groups of interview will differ because of the different circumstances, the following summarizes the format you might follow, and Figure 11.4 suggests a specimen format with the types of questions you might ask.

The format could usefully follow the structure:

1. Describe the purpose of the interview, ie follow-up evaluation of the training programme attended.
2. (Referring to the action plan) work through the types of questions contained in the questionnaire – see part one of Figure 11.1.
3. Seek any other comments relating to aspects of the action plan, particularly about any other learning achieved.
4. Seek general comments about the training programme now that the learner has had time to reflect – see the end of programme reactionnaire, part three of Figure 9.1.
5. Seek comments about the follow-up procedure and its outcomes – see part two of Figure 11.1.

FORMAT OF STRUCTURED FOLLOW-UP EVALUATION INTERVIEW

A)   Describe the reasons for, purpose and objectives of the interview that is concerned with the x training programme that the learner had followed some three months earlier.

B)   Referring to the action plan ask about:

1.   Which items of the action plan have been implemented so far?
2.   What degree of success has been achieved in respect of these items?
3.   To what factors or reasons is the success in implementing these items attributed?
4.   Which items of the action plan have not yet been implemented?
5.   Which of these items have been tried but couldn't be implemented?
6.   Why did this occur?
7.   Which items have not yet been attempted?
8.   Why have these not yet been attempted?
9.   What plans does the learner have to:
     –   attempt to rectify unsuccessful items?
     –   implement the as yet unattempted items?
10. Are there any additional plans? If so, obtain similar comments or full details.

C)   Seek any other comments relating to aspects of the action plan, particularly about any other learning achieved.

D)   Seek general comments about the training programme now that the learner has had time to reflect. The questions in part three of Figure 9.1 can form the basis for this section of the interview:

1.   Which parts of the event were found to be the most useful?
2.   Which parts of the event were found to be the least useful?
3.   Are there any parts that should have been omitted? If so, which parts and why?
4.   Is there anything that should have been added to the event? What should have been removed to make room for it?
5.   Which personal objectives were satisfied?
6.   Which personal objectives were not satisfied?
7.   Any other comments?

E)   Seek comments about the follow-up procedure and its outcomes: the questions in part two of Figure 11.1 can form the basis of this section of the interview. Confidentiality of responses and comments must be stressed and adhered to:

1.   Was a debriefing meeting with the manager held on return to work?
2.   If so, how quickly after the course did this take place?
3.   What was the nature of the debriefing meeting and its outcomes?
4.   What was the extent of the support promised by the manager?
5.   What was the extent of the support received from the manager?
6.   What was the extent of any support arranged with colleagues?
7.   What was the extent of any support received from colleagues?
8.   How valuable was the post-programme support felt to be?
9.   Any other comments?

Figure 11.4   *Format of structured follow-up evaluation interview*

This should comprise the interview, and although you should be prepared to listen to any other, wider-ranging comments the learner might make, eg about his or her further training needs, these should not be allowed to contaminate the results of the evaluation interview. If it appears that these comments are likely to be substantial, a further appointment may be advisable.

QUESTIONNAIRE OR INTERVIEW?

When circumstances give you complete freedom of choice between interviewing the learners or using an evaluation questionnaire, apart from some saving of time by using the questionnaire, which one should you use? Figure 11.5 summarizes the comparative advantages and limitations of each. The choice should be made carefully, weighing the individual items rather than looking at the number of advantages and limitations for each.

ADVANTAGES AND LIMITATIONS OF MEDIUM-TERM EVALUATION BY QUESTIONNAIRE AND INTERVIEW

QUESTIONNAIRE	INTERVIEW
Advantages	*Advantages*
Low cost – construction, postage, analysis	Interviewer able to ask supplementary and probing clarifying questions
Ideal for wide location spread of learners	More in-depth response possible
Complete sampling of trained population possible	Flexible approach according to circumstances
Speedy and timeous use	Learners accept importance of evaluation
Completely consistent format	Total response rate
Ease of analysis	
Trainer time not necessary	
Transfer to computer analysis relatively easy	
Avoids possible interviewer bias	
Avoids 'time and motion' syndrome	

Limitations	*Limitations*
Low rate of response possible without strong control mechanism	High cost
	Very high cost when locations of learners have wide spread
Requires careful design	May be seen as intrusive
Inflexible once sent	Interviewer bias possible
Questions must be clear and unambiguous	Interview skills necessary
	Analysis more time-consuming and difficult
Questions may need to be too simple	Restrictive sampling may be necessary because of time and cost – this may not be viewed as a limitation depending on size of sample and attitudes to less than total coverage
Potentially superficial completion by learners	

Figure 11.5 *Advantages and limitations of medium-term evaluation by questionnaire and interview*

Some saving of cost and time can be made by combining the two approaches, although if travel and accommodation are high features of the interview method there will be little real saving. To combine the approaches a questionnaire is sent to all participants and, when the results are analysed, if there are aspects that still require clarification, interview visits are made as appropriate. Consequently not all learners need be visited. A variation of this would be to send questionnaires to all learners and also interview a sample – this approach may, however, raise arguments about the value of sampling as opposed to full coverage, and will obviously depend on the size of the available sample or the relevant full group.

TELEPHONE FOLLOW-UP INTERVIEWS

This is an extension of the face-to-face interview approach and is an attempt to reduce costs yet still maintain the advantages of the interview. The time and cost are still obviously greater than using the questionnaire follow up, but less so than the face-to-face interview – travel with its accompanying lost time and accommodation costs are replaced by the cost of the telephone call. As a result, where the face-to-face interview approach might be restricted in numbers approached, the use of the telephone allows wider coverage, although still not as wide, perhaps, as the questionnaire. The interview can suffer to some degree, depending on the skills of the interviewer, by the absence of face-to-face interaction and possible reduction of rapport, and the interviewee may not give the same depth of attention as they would face to face.

The telephone interview will follow the same pattern as the structured, face-to-face interview with a planned pattern of appropriate questions, the responses to which can be clarified or followed up in greater depth.

Arrangements for the telephone interview may need to be more strictly controlled than for the face-to-face event:

- A telephone appointment must be made beforehand to ensure availability of the interviewee and to give them time to prepare.
- The interviewee must guarantee (as far as possible) that there will be no interruptions while the interview is taking place – the same sort of arrangement as for the face-to-face event.
- The interviewee must be alone so that there are no inhibitions about what might be said.
- The interviewer must ensure that the questions are posed clearly and that the listener has heard and understood them.
- Costs must be understood so that this does not become a factor in the pace of the interview.
- The interviewer must be aware that some people are unable to be as natural when using the phone as when in a face-to-face situation.

If the permission of the interviewee is obtained, the telephone conversation can be recorded so that the interviewer can refer back to points of the interview without having to return to the interviewee.

Although the expense is increased considerably, and I have not yet seen a medium-term evaluation interview conducted in this way, the use of long-distance telephone/television conference facilities can also be considered. Or, using modern IT methods, the interview might be conducted over local networked computer facilities or through the Internet.

CRITICAL INCIDENT ANALYSIS

Critical incident analysis or review can introduce a substantial aspect of self-reporting to the medium-term evaluation process, although the information can be gathered by the interview method, or even group discussion. The most appropriate method will depend on the customs of the organization and the degree of learner co-operation. The normal and most cost-effective method is the use of diaries, followed by an analysis of the critical incidents that these documents show.

The method used requires the learners to maintain a diary in which are written down (soon after they occur) critical incidents, particularly those relating to the learning area being evaluated, and the learner then reflects on these and makes simple judgements about them – when they happened, how they happened, why they happened, and what learning can be extracted from them.

The critical incidents can then be analysed by:

- an extraction by the learner of relevant incidents and consideration of these;
- a meeting with the line manager or a trainer who assists in the extraction, discussion and interpretation of relevant incidents;
- a group discussion during which the critical incidents are compared, discussed and analysed.

The types of incidents, how they were dealt with and an analysis of the resultant learning, although not taking the form of a complete evaluation, are valuable in this respect through the learner's involvement.

It is impossible to give any real guidance on how long a diary should be maintained for; this will depend on the complexity of the learning, the occurrence and frequency of the incidents, coverage of a range of similar but not exactly the same incidents and so on. The format of the diary is not critical – often this can be left to the learner to produce in a format that suits them, since it is effectively a self-reporting instrument. Guidance can be given to the learner about effective approaches and a suggested format is shown in Figure 11.6.

The 'diary' need not be included in the day-to-day appointments and to-do desk diary, and there are advantages in its being a separate document kept in front of the learner all the time. It can usefully take the form of separate sheets of paper, collected in a ring-binder.

LEARNING LOGS

Learning Logs were described in Chapter 7 as instruments designed to help the learners remember, recall, share and reinforce their learning during the training programme. Their use as interim validation instruments was also considered. Similarly they can become part of a person's continuing professional development after the formal programme and as such can be valuable post-programme evaluation tools. An example of a Learning Log was included as Figure 7.12.

A CRITICAL INCIDENT DIARY

DATE .... DIARY SHEET NUMBER ....

Include in this diary what you see as critical incidents concerned with your work and your relationships with your colleagues, particularly those relating to the learning you have achieved from the training programme .... , although you need not restrict yourself to this area. Include incidents of both a satisfactory and unsatisfactory nature.

1. What happened; how did it happen; when did it happen; who was involved; and why did it happen?
2. What was the outcome of the incident? Was it satisfactory or unsatisfactory?
3. Who or what was responsible for this outcome?
4. If the outcome was satisfactory, what have you learned from the processes that made it so?
5. If it was unsatisfactory, what made it so and what learning can you take from this?
6. Was the incident relevant to the training you followed? If so, did the training help you to cope with the incident? To what extent?
7. Did the incident expose any further training needs you might have?

Figure 11.6 *A critical incident diary*

At the end of a training programme during which Learning Logs have been completed, used for review and accepted by the learners as useful instruments, they should be encouraged to continue the use of the logs after the programme as a record of part of their continuous learning and development. Incidents from which they have learned something should be entered in their continuing log with comments that effectively form an action plan. These entries and plans can be considered at an evaluation review as helpful indicators of the implementation and continuation of their learning in very much the same way as the critical incident diary.

REPERTORY GRID

The repertory grid has a number of uses, including that of evaluation. It is, however, a technique that is complex and time-consuming to use, and its application in evaluation (apart from perhaps in research) occurs only infrequently. In order to obtain the maximum benefit from its use, the practitioner should preferably be trained and experienced in the technique. Mention of it is included here for the sake of completeness.

A repertory grid compares effective and ineffective behaviours, through which behaviour analysis, based on an acceptable model of behaviour, can be used more effectively. The technique is derived from the personal construct work (each person's unique framework for understanding the world) of George Kelly (1953), to whose work you are referred if you wish to try out the technique. Examples of the practical application of the technique in evaluation are described in Leslie Rae (1991) and Peter Honey (1979).

LONGER-TERM EVALUATION

The effects of training and development programmes and their consequent immediate learning and medium-term implementation do not necessarily remain over a longer period. Time and situations allow the individuals to forget the techniques and methods learned, or allow them to slip back to the pre-training state of 'unconscious incompetence'. This last-named state is part of a useful method of expressing the movement and/or change of an individual over a period of time, usually as a result of training.

THE COMPETENCE STEPLADDER

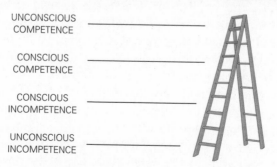

UNCONSCIOUS COMPETENCE

CONSCIOUS COMPETENCE

CONSCIOUS INCOMPETENCE

UNCONSCIOUS INCOMPETENCE

Learning is the process of change and can be demonstrated by the competence steps.

People performing a task or role may be doing so without complete competence, but they are unaware of these deficiencies until by a variety of mechanisms they may be made aware of them and so pass up the steps to the area of conscious incompetence. As a result of taking some learning action they become capable and competent in the process, but have to perform it consciously and deliberately. Full implementation, practice and performance at work raise the level to the top step of unconscious competence, where learning has been achieved and the task is performed effectively without too much conscious thought. All too easily, however, unconscious competence can slip back to unconscious incompetence!

Learning programmes set out to achieve this change, at least to the borderline between conscious and unconscious competence, and longer-term evaluation has as one of its objectives the checking of maintained competence.

LONGER-TERM EVALUATION FORMAT

Longer-term evaluation is performed later than medium-term evaluation, usually between nine months and a year following the end of the training programme. The approaches used for the medium-term stage apply equally at this later stage, but concentrate on the long-term implementation of the learning, and in particular the items included on the action plan. There would seem to be little value in seeking further information about the training itself at this stage as this might have been obtained at the medium-term evaluation and, 12 months after the event, the learners' memories will be hazy with intervening work and possibly further training.

The evaluation can be carried out by either the line manager or, perhaps if the medium-term evaluation was performed by the trainer, by either a face-to-face visit or by telephone interview, again by the trainer. If everything seems to be well and the learning achieved is still being implemented (if appropriate), the evaluation process is over. If, however, unforeseen or undesirable changes have taken place, an investigation (perhaps in the form of a training need analysis or performance analysis) will need to be carried out. The line manager can take a wider view in this respect and will usually be in a more effective position to carry out this analysis.

The longer-term evaluation completes the practical evaluation process, but essential in the enquiry is the question of the value effectiveness of the training to the organization – is it worth it? This will be considered in the next chapter as the conclusions formed about this will be the most significant aspect of the evaluation report, which will be considered in Chapter 13. But without the various stages of the evaluation process discussed so far, assessment of worth will not be possible.

12

—

Cost and Value Effectiveness

It has been shown that the major objectives of validation and evaluation are:

- validation of the achievement of the training programme objectives;
- validation of the achievement of the learner's objectives;
- evaluation of the implementation of the action plan and other learning.

But these, important and essential though they may be, do not exhaust the potential or indeed the requirements of the evaluation process. In addition:

- it must be shown, as far as possible, that the training and learning achieved have been done so with cost and value effectiveness;
- the results of the evaluation process should be reported to the sponsors of the training and the evaluation.

COST EFFECTIVENESS

The costing of training programmes consists of inputs and outputs. Cost inputs consider one side of the financial equation, the cost of the programmes, and whether this has been the most economical and effective approach. On the face of it, this would seem to be simple and straightforward accounting, but within the majority of quantitative aspects there is also a minority of qualitative aspects about which broad assessment only is possible.

The major headings included in cost inputs are:

> - ■ FIXED CAPITAL COSTS
> - ■ MAINTENANCE OR WORKING CAPITAL COSTS
> - ■ ADMINISTRATIVE COSTS
> - ■ TRAINER COSTS
> - ■ DIRECT TRAINING COSTS
> - ■ EXTERNAL AGENT COSTS
> - ■ TRAINEE COSTS

Without this information the organization will have no idea of such details as:

- ■ How many trainers must it employ to perform the training required?
- ■ How much does a trainer cost?
- ■ What is the total cost of the training to the organization?
- ■ What is the cost of a training day? How many training days can the organization afford?
- ■ What is the comparable cost of an open learning package and can the organization afford the requisite number of packages?
- ■ What is the cost of training in relation to production or provision of services costs?
- ■ Is the training worth the expenditure?

Fixed capital costs

These are costs that are relatively permanent and regular and are fixed over a period of time, say a year. They can include parts of the organization's building(s) that can be fully or partly attributable to training purposes in terms of:

- ■ building cost and depreciation;
- ■ building taxes;
- ■ fuel and water provision;
- ■ fixtures and fittings depreciation;
- ■ other fixed services – computer links;
- ■ equipment – computers, typewriters, OHPs, videos etc;
- ■ provision of a training resource centre and/or library;
- ■ transport.

Maintenance or working capital costs

Maintenance or working capital costs include:

- consumables – eg stationery;
- routine maintenance and repair contracts;
- other materials used during the training by trainers and trainees.

Administrative costs

Administrative costs include such items as:

- cleaning costs;
- support service staff accommodation, materials and salaries attributable to training-related duties;
- telephone and utility charges attributable to the training function;
- computer time charges where appropriate.

Trainer costs

Trainer costs include:

- costs of employing a training manager (where relevant) or apportioned costs, and the partly attributable costs of more senior managers with some responsibility for the training function;
- trainer and/or programme designers' and writers' salaries and expenses, whether actually engaged on training activities or not;
- continued training and development of training staff;
- professional fees for training staff;
- subscriptions to professional journals and purchase of training resources;
- licence fees.

Direct training costs

Costs incurred directly in relation to the training itself include fees and expenses for guest speakers.

External agent costs

External agent costs include:

- consultant fees and expenses;
- external course fees and expenses;
- purchase of open learning programmes if not accounted for elsewhere.

Trainee costs

Trainee costs include:

- apportionment of salary for period of travelling to and from and attending the training programme;
- cost of pre-programme action with line manager (also apportioned to line manager costs);
- travel and accommodation costs;
- cost of replacement staff, where relevant;
- opportunity costs.

The last-named can be the most difficult cost to determine, as it is concerned with the value of the work lost owing to the absence of the individual. This of course can be complicated if the work is left for the individual's return, resulting in a delay cost. In many cases this will have to be a guesstimate cost, although some organizations claim they use a formula to determine this opportunity cost. It may be possible to cost some jobs in this way with a relationship to loss of production, but it will always be a highly subjective assessment.

Figure 12.1 suggests an exercise for costing training.

COST ANALYSIS

The figures obtained under the headings described above can be used to produce a summary statement from which a number of conclusions about the cost of training can be made. These will include:

- Direct cost of a training programme
- Direct cost of the total training function
- Cost of the training function per individual within the organization
- Cost of the training programme per learner

AN EXERCISE IN TRAINING COSTING

Fixed capital costs

Parts of the organization's building(s) that can be fully or partly attributable to training purposes in terms of:

- building cost and depreciation ....
- building taxes ....
- fuel and water provision ....
- fixtures and fittings depreciation ....
- other fixed services – computer links ....
- equipment – computers, typewriters, OHPs, videos etc ....
- provision of a training resource centre and/or library ....
- transport. ....

Maintenance or working capital costs

- consumables – eg stationery ....
- routine maintenance and repair contracts ....
- other materials used during the training by trainers and trainees. ....

Administrative costs

- cleaning ....
- support service staff accommodation, materials and salaries attributable to training-related duties ....
- telephone and utility charges attributable to the training function ....
- computer time charges where appropriate. ....

Trainer costs

- costs of employing a training manager, where relevant, or apportioned costs, and the partly attributable costs of more senior managers with some responsibility for the training function ....
- trainer and/or programme designers' and writers' salaries and expenses ....
- continued training and development of training staff ....
- professional fees for training staff ....
- subscriptions to professional journal and purchase of training resources ....
- licence fees. ....

Figure 12.1 *An exercise in training costing*

Direct training costs

■ fees and expenses for guest speakers, where
  relevant. ....

External agent costs

■ consultant fees and expenses ....
■ external course fees and expenses ....
■ purchase of open learning programmes if not
  accounted for elsewhere. ....

Trainee costs

■ apportionment of salary for period of travelling to
  and from and attending the training programme ....
■ cost of pre-programme action with line manager
  (also apportioned to line manager costs) ....
■ travel and accommodation costs ....
■ cost of replacement staff, where relevant ....
■ opportunity costs. ....

Figure 12.1 *An exercise in training costing (continued)*

The costing of a specific programme is interesting and useful, but the
major benefits emerge when comparing particular periods of training.
In comparisons of this kind it is not essential that the figures are
completely accurate, provided the same calculations and methods of
calculation are used consistently.

The cost per trainer

If all the costs of one training are added together to produce an overall
cost, which is then divided by the number of people contributing to
the training – trainers, training manager, administration staff, external
speakers – the resulting figure is one of unit cost. The following example
demonstrates this calculation.

1. Sum of all costs for year **A** with a training function
   staff of eight £750,000
2. Unit cost per trainer ($^1/_8$) = £94,000

This of course is a very simplistic cost statement, as it does not take
into account the number of learners on each programme – the greater

the number of people trained, the lower the unit cost – or a number of other factors. However, even in this form, comparative information can be obtained.

1. Sum of all costs for year **B** with a training function staff of eight £900,000
2. Unit cost per trainer ($\frac{1}{8}$) = £112,500

However, in reality

1. Sum of all costs for year **B** with a training function staff of eight but with a cost-of-living index increase of 8 per cent £972,000
2. Unit cost per trainer ($\frac{1}{8}$) = £121,500

However, the actual rise from £750,000 to £972,000 equates to an increase of about 22 per cent. There may of course be very valid reasons for this increase, but in the first instance an assessor will be alerted to a change in the costing.

Cost per learner and per event

Similar calculations can be used for other analyses.

1. Sum of all costs for year **A** with 9 000 learners passing through 600 courses £750,000
2. Cost per learner = £83
3. Cost per course = £1,250

If, however, in the following year:

1. Sum of all costs for year **B** with 12,600 learners passing through 900 courses £900,000
2. Cost per learner = £71
3. Cost per course = £1,000

In spite of the demonstrated increase of 22 per cent.

Learners per course

A useful analysis is to cost the training in terms of the number of learners who have attended the events and make a comparison of these costs with variations. We have seen above the effect of increasing the number of learners and courses, but different variations can also occur. Let us take the example where the total costs obtained are £900,000 for 12 600 learners attending 900 courses – a cost of £71 per learner and £1000 per course. It may be that the organization has decreed that the costs of training must be reduced, but the level of training must not vary too greatly. If the number of courses is reduced with the course:learner ratio remaining the same, costs will be reduced but learning will suffer. One approach might be to increase the number of learners on each course – we assume that the original courses were designed for maximum benefit with a particular number of learners on each course. If the original number per course was 14 and the increase was to 18 – an increase of about a third – there may be some diminution of the learning; this could be within containable bounds, although it may require the use of less effective training methods, for example more input sessions and fewer activities. The organization's requirements, however, would be achieved – in this case we would have a total cost of £900,000 for 16 200 learners on the 900 courses. Of course, there would need to be some other cost adjustments in a full cost analysis – increases in the learner costs of salary and opportunity attributions – but the net result would be a lower cost per learner.

The increase in course population causes a particularly noticeable effect when we consider training by external providers. If we disregard all costings other than the provider's fees (which might be £2 500), when the normal course attendance is eight the unit learner cost is £312. An increase to a usually satisfactory total of 12 decreases the unit learner cost to £208; and, albeit not fully desirable from a training/ learning point of view, if the participants are increased to 15, the cost per learner falls to £167. The provider's fees remain the same, but a real saving is obtained by a reduction in the number of required courses and other costs attributable to fewer courses. Care has to be taken that the external provider does not require a greater fee for the higher numbers of participants.

There will obviously be some reduction of the quality in the training/ learning if the course population is increased to too great an extent, and this must be weighed against the cost reductions demanded.

There are, of course, ways of obtaining a reduction in training costs, while retaining the extent of training, other than increasing the number of learners on a course. Open learning, once the initial capital cost of the packages is taken into account, is frequently less costly than direct training courses, particularly where the latter include accommodation for the training, the trainers and the learners. Naturally this cost is evened out by multiple use, but care must be taken when deciding to use such packages that the approach is the most appropriate, effective, and so on.

VALUE EFFECTIVENESS

The guidance given above on obtaining the costs of training is but one side of the equation, and has taken no account of the *value* obtained from the training. This covers the increase in knowledge, skills and attitudes; the increase in work capacities; the decrease in undesirable practices and events; but above all an increase in the business 'bottom line'. Cost analysis leading to an assessment of cost effectiveness is not simple – it is not always easy to obtain the financial information or produce real attribution or apportionment. But obtaining the value of the training is much more difficult, so much so that some people suggest that it is impossible to attain. It is frequently the principal argument used against evaluation – based on the so-called 'soft/hard' benefits – in that evaluators cannot provide incontrovertible evidence of an increase in hard benefits to the business. It is difficult to counter this argument as, although there can be significant concrete evidence for some learning events, more training results are subjective (not only in the training area, but also at work).

Certainly it is frequently impossible to obtain a cost/value effectiveness statement in completely quantitative terms, but this is not necessarily an argument not to try. In many, if not the majority, of cases it may be necessary to accept subjective and qualitative assessments, perhaps relying on a consistency of approach to produce acceptable, comparative results.

Some aspects are *easier* to assess for value, and the areas in which change might be observed following training and development programmes include aspects of the back-at-work implementation of the learning, although care must be taken in attributing all changes to the training. It is so easy for contamination to take place – the learner might have read something since returning from the course; economic pressures may have changed attitudes; the weather might have improved (!) and so on. Some of these changed aspects include the following.

Time usage

Better use of time means that meetings are kept to time and are time effective; appointments are kept promptly; reports etc are submitted at the due time, and so on.

Work practices

These can be suggested by a stricter adherence to health and safety practices or following effective operating procedures (perhaps modified following a programme that looked at the existing procedures). These changes might be observed at operative, supervisory or management levels. In the latter two, assessment might be made from observation of an improvement in checks made that were not made previously; a closer support of subordinates in their work practices; and, linking with the next category, an increase in output and reduction in waste.

Output of products or services

This is visible in an increase in the amount of work produced, sales or other visits made etc. Positive results of this nature may be achieved following programmes aimed at effective supervisory or management practices; project management; team development; problem-solving and so on.

Costs

Many industrial and commercial costs are attributable to people – their efficiency, interpersonal relationships, discipline, attendance, leaving and recruitment and other personnel matters. Any changes may be the results of programmes concerned with people skills, interviewing techniques, interpersonal skills, effective working etc.

People

Team development, interpersonal skills and people relationship programmes might result in improvements of these aspects in the people undertaking tasks – how well they get on with each other, how much support they give each other, how well they listen, and to what extent they work as a team rather than a collection of individuals.

Individual development

A number of programmes aim to increase people's creative ability, help them to present themselves in more favourable lights, demonstrate their promotability and, in general, be more effective and 'wider' people.

Quality of products and services

This can be assessed from a reduction in the number of rejects of products and customer complaints; reduced operating costs; increased levels of evaluation (!); increased business.

Improvements in the organizational climate and culture

Without doubt this is the most difficult to assess. Fewer resignations and discharges, less sick leave, increased production and a reduction in customer complaints – these and other indicators may give the opportunity to assess a change, but all are highly subjective, particularly when confirmation of a direct link with a training/learning programme is attempted.

OBJECTIVE AND SUBJECTIVE ANALYSIS

The examples of assessable change described above vary in their ease of implementation. Changes or results can be described as 'hard' or 'soft', depending on the extent of objectivity and ease of observation, The so-called 'hard' changes are the *easier* to observe and analyse and in the list above are more likely to include:

- the use of time in observable situations;
- some work practices;
- product output;
- product quality.

The 'soft' changes are in much more subjective areas that are more complicated to observe and analyse, and are more likely to be in the qualitative areas of behaviour than the observable task areas. They would include:

- some work practices that are not easy to observe or define;
- management, supervisory or team 'skills';
- relationships with people;
- individual development;
- output of services as opposed to products;
- quality of services rendered as opposed to products made;
- improvements in organizational climate and culture.

Whether the comparison is objective or subjective, it must always be made in the light of the pre-training situation, otherwise you are not measuring anything. Remember that the pre-training position might be zero. Such a case occurs where the training being considered for evaluation is one for new entrants to an occupation of which they have no previous experience. Some minimal on-the-job training had been given prior to more effective training in a formalized setting and the following example sets out the proposed progress as a result of the training and the measures to evaluate its success and value after the event.

Area of change	Pre-training performance	Post-training objective	Actual post-training results
Number of widgets rejected at quality control point	10% of production	1% or less of production	0.5% of production

A successful result such as this, if it is measured immediately after the training, can be assumed to relate directly to the training, although there will still be some other aspects involved – motivation, fear of discharge, change of staff etc.

The 'softer' type of changes, which have no quantitative measures, are more difficult to assess for success, but if a model exists against which the learners were assessed before the training programme, the model observation can be used again for post-training, work-environment practice.

Although in either type of change it may be possible to observe and analyse the movement, to put a price on these improvements is more difficult. The simplest case may be the effective training of a worker to do a job that if it were not done at all would not bring in any money. When the operative is trained and producing, the products are sold for a certain price from which operating costs must be taken, leaving a profit – the bottom-line value effectiveness of the training. Would that it were always that simple!

As always the caveat must be that there is no absolute guarantee that any improvement or change is completely, or even minimally, due to the training programme, but any changes may be an *indication* of success along these lines. This is not to suggest that no attempt should be made to assess a cost or undertake other value analysis of training – quite the reverse. But the problems and difficulties must be recognized and care taken in attributing success or failure and a change in cost and/or value. It may be necessary to accept the subjective views and estimates suggested earlier because the area being considered is too subjective in itself to be *measured*.

Assessments at this stage are principally concerned with evaluation (the total benefits) rather than the simple validation of the training programme itself. A significant number of people might be involved in the evaluation and it may be necessary to involve people from multi-disciplines. The person responsible – senior management, line manager, training manager or trainer – must decide to what extent resources must be provided for this (often extensive and expensive) exercise; whether the time involved (time that may be disproportionate to the time taken on the training itself) should be expended; and to what extent the degrees of subjectivity and objectivity should be accepted.

ASSESSING THE RETURN ON INVESTMENT

A number of publications that include comments on evaluation contain a variety of formulae and equations that claim to assess the cost–value effectiveness results of training and development. One *apparently* straightforward and simple equation is represented by:

$$\frac{\text{Financial value of change/effect achieved}}{\text{Cost of training process}} \times \frac{100}{1} = \% \text{ business return on investment}$$

It will be obvious from all the comments made previously in this chapter that this equation requires so much detail in the first part of the equation (both above and below the line), which may be impossible to obtain in a quantitative or objective form, that in most cases it is too simplistic to be of much use.

GUIDELINES FOR VALUE-EFFECTIVE ANALYSIS

The following summarizes the guidelines that should help in this difficult area.

1. Don't be put off by the apparent, or real, difficulties and subjective nature of the areas to be assessed – try something.
2. In subjective assessment try for comparisons with similar events under similar conditions.

3. Seek the views – albeit subjective ones – of others. For example, ask for the critical views of customers, internal and external.
4. Compare results against models or even concepts when the areas are completely subjective in nature.
5. Only gather information or data that you will be able to use, however interesting or easy to obtain other 'data' might be.
6. Ask the line manager of the learners before the events for their estimate of how much it will be worth to them and their operation to have an effective person. After the training evaluate the success and ask the line manager whether their initial estimates have been achieved.
7. Seek, but do not necessarily take as positive proof, organizational effects linked to the training areas – increased productivity, decreased absences, discipline incidents, grievances etc. Link these to other evaluation processes to ensure that contamination has not occurred.

13

Analysing and Reporting on Evaluation Data

ANALYSING THE EVALUATION RESULTS

The evaluation process itself is not the end of the story. If nothing is done with the results of the evaluation (usually produced in the form of data), the exercise and the time and resources involved will have been wasted. In some cases the next step may be simple, because of the small amount of data, but in other cases – extensive evaluation instruments used with a large number of learners and over a large number of programmes – the amount of data can be considerable.

There is a variety of analysis methods designed to cope with this data, ranging from the simplest possible to a complex approach involving the manipulation of hundreds (if not thousands) of bits of data. These approaches include:

- simple examination;
- test marking;
- text comparison;
- data and text comparison;
- extended data comparison.

All these approaches assume that both pre- and post-programme evaluation methods have been used to some extent. If they have not, analysis means little and only highly subjective views can be formed. For example, if only an end of course 'happiness' sheet is used, all that can be done is to look at the sheets and say 'it looks as if *they* are saying that *they* have enjoyed the course and that something of value has been learned' – not a very valid consideration if your boss has asked you to prove that your training programme is worth continuing in cost and resource terms!

THE SCORING ANALYSIS APPROACH

This simple analytical approach can be used with the simplest validation approach – an end of course validation questionnaire – which asks for a learning score and/or other session or opinion scores. The 'examination', at its simplest, consists of the trainer who conducted the programme looking at the questionnaires and forming an impression of the responses. The impression will be gained from a comparison of the range of scores given for the level of learning – *'most of the scores seem to be in the 4 to 5 range, with one or two 6s, so that seems OK'* and *'the learning statements seem to cover the major objectives I had constructed for the programme'*.

This type of 'validation' is obviously highly subjective, and not very satisfactory, but is common none the less. A simple extension of this can produce results that can be used for comparison purposes over an extended programme or number of programmes. A simple chart can be produced in which the learning scores are entered, as shown in Figure 13.1.

Name of learner	Learning score	Name of learner	Learning score
a	6	g	5
b	5	h	4
c	5	j	6
d	4	k	5
e	6	l	5
f	5	m	6

Figure 13.1 *Scoring analysis table*

The 'average' score for the programme is 5.2, ie the sum of the learning scores divided by the number of learners. This figure can be compared with the average scores for other, similar programmes and will indicate whether achievement of the programme objectives is remaining constant or changing with time.

A significant change of the scoring with time will be a signal for investigation. During a run of events that produce a common scoring of about 5, if one event shows an average score of 3, with each learner distributing their scores about this figure, the immediate assumption must not be made that the programme has gone wrong. The reasons for the change are almost endless, and include:

- a course made up of learners who should not have been attending;
- a catastrophic environmental fault;
- a new trainer involved who had been ineffectively prepared.

THE SCORING AND TEXT ANALYSIS APPROACH

My comments throughout on validation questionnaires have been that scoring tables are not sufficient for effective evaluation, and can be dangerous. This danger can be reduced and the value of the questionnaire increased if, in addition to the scoring requested, the learners are also *required* to make comments about their scoring. An example of this type of questionnaire is demonstrated in Figure 9.1. Analysis in this approach starts with the construction of a table as shown in Figure 13.1. This numerical analysis is then supported with a summary of the textual comments, which can be compared with the desired training or learning objectives.

If the learners demonstrate that, apart from the knowledge and skills they possessed at the start of the programme, they have achieved the 'learning points' listed, there is an indication that the programme has been successful in helping the learners to learn. Comparison in such cases can be relatively simple. Figure 13.2 demonstrates a hypothetical comparison table of this nature, based on part of the learning objectives of an effective communication programme.

A listing of the negative comments can also be made for post-event consideration. If the Figure 9.1 type of questionnaire is used and the learning scoring is in the range 4 to 1, the learners are asked to comment why they have given that scoring. The responses can again be summarized, as shown in Figure 13.3.

The frequency of the comments will demonstrate their significance – if, on a course of 12 members, eight or more make similar comments, notice must be taken of this. Comments made by perhaps only one or two participants have to be considered in a different way. It may be that the trainer must make a value judgement on the importance or significance of the nature of the comment, or because one learner has commented in a particular way, for that learner there were problems. This may be significant – bear in mind that a particular aspect *can* cause problems for some learners.

Effective communication course	
Learning objectives	**Learner statements**
Interacting effectively with others	'I now know that I have difficulties in relating to others' 'I can now relate to others more effectively by seeking their views rather than always giving mine'
Knowledge of the different types of assertiveness	'I realize now that my approach to people has always been aggressive whereas it should be assertive'
Skill in demonstrating the different types of assertiveness	'During the course I tried not being aggressive with others and found that it worked. I shall try this out with my colleagues at work when I return'
Giving effective praise to others	'I still have problems in telling others that they have done a good job, but I tried it out fairly successfully on the course and shall continue trying to do so'
Accepting criticism from others	'I have always fought against being criticized, but I shall now look for real messages in any criticism I receive in future'

Figure 13.2 *Positive text recording*

Comments	**Frequency**
1. The pace of the course was too fast to take in the material	|||
2. I couldn't understand the differences between the forms of assertiveness and it wasn't explained clearly	⊞⊞
3. The training room was too warm for comfort	|||

Figure 13.3 *Negative text recording*

GRAPHICAL REPRESENTATION

The computer can usefully be introduced in the analysis of the completed evaluation instruments and, instead of a manually prepared table, a spreadsheet can be constructed from the data which can be easily updated and manipulated. New figures can be added to the spreadsheet, automatically replacing and updating the original ones, and formulae for mathematical calculations can be built in. For example, in a chart of scores with rows of learners and columns of separate events, a formula can be included at the end of a row to sum the figures in that row and produce an average. Similarly, an averaged summation can be produced for each learner in each activity or session scored. A typical chart would appear as shown in Figure 13.4.

LEARNER	SESSION 1	SESSION 2	SESSION 3	SESSION 4	Sum sessions 1–4/4
a	5	6	6	5	5.5
b	4	5	5	4	4.5
c	6	5	6	6	5.75
. . .					
x	5	6	6	4	5.25
y	6	6	6	5	5.75
z	5	5	6	4	5
26 learners	Sum of all rows/26	Sum of all rows/26	Sum of all rows/26	Sum of all rows/26	Sum of all rows/26

Figure 13.4 *Spreadsheet chart*

Too much detail can confuse rather than help, and most people are able to interpret a graphical representation of the figures more easily. Again, the production of such information is simple with the computer. The abbreviated figures shown in Figure 13.4 would appear in graphical format as shown in Figure 13.5.

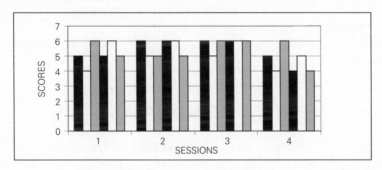

Figure 13.5 *Graphical representation*

CHANGE ANALYSIS

When more than a simple analysis of end of programme data is involved, the resulting tables and charts become much more complex. In the case of a pre- and post-programme assessment, the two questionnaires used would probably each include about 15 questions – ie 15 questions x 2 questionnaires x (say) 12 participants = 360 items of data for each course or event for analysis. If the three-test approach was used a third questionnaire would be introduced, producing another 180 items of data. If we include the line manager in the pre- and post-event assessment, a further 360 items would need to be included, a total of 900 items of data. This final figure would of course be increased by the number of similar programmes to be analysed and compared.

Producing an analytical report from such data would normally require the evaluator to compare the pre-event score for each item on the questionnaire with the same item on the post-event questionnaire and note the difference, ie the change in knowledge, skill or attitude over the programme. The basic data could again be plotted on the spreadsheet with the use of formulae to calculate the changes – this also makes the introduction of the third questionnaire in the three-test relatively simple. The results could then be exhibited in table or graphical chart form as shown in Figures 13.4 and 13.5.

ANALYSING TEST RESULTS

There is a significant difference between evaluation using objective tests of learning of knowledge and skills and the more subjective approaches only possible when assessing people skills, attitudes and behaviours. More disciplined analyses can be applied to the more objective forms of testing. Statistical analysis is a complex and difficult subject, one which few trainers will have the time or the skill to perform fully. There are, however, some simpler methods that will give at least an indication of the validity of the tests and their results.

The two most common approaches of this form of analysis are *location* and *dispersion*.

LOCATION ANALYSIS

This approach identifies the middle position of results and provides what is commonly referred to as the 'average'. There are, however, three types of 'average':

1. **The average or mean** – this is calculated by summing all the individual data items and dividing by the number of items. The mean can then be expressed in the raw numbers or as a percentage of the summation. For example, if for a set of test questions the resulting data was 6, 6, 5, 4, 6, 5, 5, 6, 6, 6, 5, 4, 6, 5, 6, 5, 6, 6, 3, 5, the mean would be: 5.3, ie 106 (total of scores)/20 (number of scores).
2. **The median** – if the scores are arranged in numerical order, the median is the middle value of the set of scores.
3. **The mode** – this is the score value that occurs most frequently in the set of data.

When it is necessary to examine the average in greater depth (for example, in research) the median numerical sequence would be used. From the data arranged in numerical order, the lower and upper quartiles can be calculated. The lower quartile is obtained from the score data below which 25 per cent of the score items fall and above which 75 per cent occur; the upper quartile is obtained similarly from the value above which 25 per cent of the score items occur and below which 75 per cent fall. But, in the majority of cases, a simple mean is all that is necessary to indicate the level of test success, the other approaches being used more by researchers and external experts considering evaluation.

In statistical analysis, validation has a particular meaning and has a link with another measure of reliability. Practical analysis will probably involve little more than comparing the mean results of a number of event tests. Wild variations will suggest investigation as described earlier and will relate to either an invalid and unreliable testing approach, or problems relating to the training itself.

DISPERSION ANALYSIS

The problems raised by the location analysis described above can often be further refined by examining the data dispersal – certainly this will identify cases where there are obviously problems related either to the testing or the training, and will lead to the need to investigate further.

Although there are a number of dispersion measures, of the three most common – range, inter-quartile range and standard deviation – the range is the one most often used in practical evaluation. This measure, at its simplest, shows the lowest and highest values in the scoring data set. A wide range again suggests investigation of either the testing and scoring procedure, or the training itself.

TRAINING AND DEVELOPMENT ASSESSMENTS

The final stage of the validation/evaluation/assessment process for a training and development programme will depend on a number of factors, including the requirements or demands of the stakeholders (senior management), and the availability of resources to carry out further investigation, analysis and reporting. The first factor will be the most significant as, depending on the importance given to evaluation by senior management, any problems of resources could be resolved.

A training and development assessment is substantially wider than programme evaluation, although this is an essential part of the process, providing much of the information on which the assessment will be based. Three different levels can be approached, each treated separately if necessary:

- the training and development events;
- the training and development programme;
- the administration of the training and development.

The content of these levels has an obvious relationship to the training quintet referred to in Chapter 2.

ASSESSING THE TRAINING AND DEVELOPMENT EVENTS

The evidence on which the stage of an assessment will be based has been provided by the validation and evaluation activities of a particular training course or package. These can be supplemented by interviews by the assessor with the trainers involved and with the learners (or a representative sample) and their line managers. The latter interactions can be linked to the medium-term evaluation activities.

The principal questions for which validated responses will be necessary for the assessment are shown in Figure 13.6.

ASSESSING THE TRAINING AND DEVELOPMENT PROGRAMME

Individual training events can exist as single, stand-alone events; as part of a number of similar events designed to satisfy a major training

1. What were the broad aims of the event? How were these established?
2. Was an effective training needs identification and analysis performed? By whom?
3. What were the terminal objectives identified for the event? Were these related to task or behaviour, or both?
4. Have the objectives for the event been altered at any time? If so, why and with what result?
5. How were the learner participants for the event identified and by whom? Was this an effective process?
6. What is the demand for this particular training event? To what extent can the demand be met?
7. To what extent did the learners' line managers take relevant/ requested pre-event action? (For example, ensuring that any pre-training projects were performed and a pre-event briefing meeting was held.)
8. Was the learning event the most appropriate one for the learners' needs?
9. If the event only failed these needs minimally, what needs to be done to remedy the failings?
10. If there were major failings of the learners' needs, what must be done to remedy these and to what extent?
11. Are there any plans being made for implementing these remedies?
12. Were the training aids, training activities and handouts of sufficient quality?
13. Did the trainer(s) perform input sessions and facilitate training activities in a satisfactory manner?
14. Were guest speakers of acceptable quality? If not, what action has been taken?
15. What was the extent and nature of any validation and evaluation measures performed?
16. How were they undertaken? Was time during the event available for them? If not, what action is being taken to provide this?
17. What is the summarized result of these processes?
18. What (subjective) views do the relevant trainers hold about the success or otherwise of the event?
19. Do the trainers have any views or opinions about the event that are not demonstrated by the validation and evaluation instruments?
20. Has this event been assessed on a previous occasion? What conclusions emerged from that assessment? Were any recommendations acted upon? With what results?

Figure 13.6 *Key assessment questions about the training event*

need; or as a singular event within a series of integrated events forming a logical programme (eg a supervisor or management development programme).

The questions suggested for the first two of these situations have been described above. When a complete programme is being considered for assessment the process will usually consist of two stages – assessment of the individual events and assessment of the programme as a whole. Figure 13.7 summarizes the principal, *additional* questions that need to be asked about the programme for assessment purposes. Much of the information will be contained in the assessment of the individual events that constitute the programme, but these parts need to be brought together for an assessment of the whole programme. Some of the individual event questions can also be modified for the programme as a whole.

---

1. Were all the constituent parts of the programme in line with:
   - the identified training needs?
   - the aims and objectives of the programme?
   - necessary parts of the programme?
2. Is there a satisfactory balance of specific topics within the programme? Are the relevant degrees of topic importance reflected in the programme?
3. Are any changes (modifications, additions or removal of topics and/or events) necessary?
4. Are the resources available – trainers and materials – sufficient to carry out the programme effectively?
5. Are the trainers sufficiently capable and developed to carry out the programme effectively? To what extent do the trainers need to be able to be involved in a number of elements of the programme? Is there any plan existing to extend these abilities, if necessary?
6. To what extent have the costs and values of the programme been investigated? How were these identified and by whom? What results do they show?
7. Does the cost analysis show that the organization can continue to afford to provide a budget for the programme? Are any financial modifications needed?
8. Does the value analysis show that the organization can continue to afford to provide a budget for the programme? Are any financial modifications needed?
9. From the cost/value investigation results, is continuation of the programme recommended?

Figure 13.7 *Additional assessment questions relating to the programme*

ASSESSING THE ADMINISTRATION OF TRAINING AND DEVELOPMENT

There is more to training than the up-front, highly visible events, and the administration of the training has an important part to play in its success or failure. Consequently an essential part of the assessment is an investigation into these back-up services. Included in this definition are the actions of the course administration department, training manager and the senior management group. Some of the key questions in this area are included in Figure 13.8.

Administration

1. Were all relevant accommodation requirements provided, including both training resources (for example, fixed whiteboards) and residential requirements (where necessary)?
2. Were all training materials provided, eg handouts, training aids, course stationery?
3. Did all participants receive the requisite course advisory material and in good time?
4. Were all attempts made to ensure a maximum number of participants? Were dropouts promptly and effectively replaced?
5. How effective and interactive is the relationship between the administration department and the training staff?

Training manager

1. To what extent did the training manager support the training staff in the provision of the training programme?
2. To what extent did the training manager require validation and evaluation approaches?
3. What level of interest and action did the training manager take in the validation and evaluation results?
4. Did the training manager ensure that the training staff were developed in both their professional and technical skills?
5. What degree of liaison is there between the training manager and the sponsors or major clients (eg senior management)?
6. To what extent is the training manager involved in early discussions and decisions on training and development with the sponsor or senior management group?
7. Has the training manager produced a training plan and is the relevant programme in line with the aims and objectives of this plan?

Line manager

1. How aware are they of the facilities offered to them and their staff for training and development?
2. To what extent have they taken up these facilities?
3. What views have line managers formed of the quality of training of their staff?
4. Do they feel the training is cost and value effective? If not, why not and what changes would they recommend?
5. How effective do they feel the call-up and other administrative arrangements are?
6. Do they practise pre-event and post-event briefing discussions with the learners?
7. If not, why not?
8. To what extent are they able to support the implementation of the person's learning?
9. To what extent are they involved in the medium- and long-term evaluation?
10. If to a limited extent only, would they want greater involvement?
11. Has the training event/programme satisfied the needs of them and their staff?
12. Have they identified any deficiencies in the programme?
13. Have they identified any shortcomings with the trainers on the relevant programmes?
14. Have any constraints made it difficult for them to allow their staff to take part in the events/programmes? How can these be resolved?
15. What additional help or support would they want from the training department?
16. How willing are they to become involved in the training planning and design, its implementation and its evaluation?

The learner

1. What is their overall impression of the effectiveness of the event/programme?
2. What is their overall impression of the value of the course to them?
3. How well did the training meet their needs? If not, or if not fully, what was not met? Should it have been? How could it have been met?

4. What views did they have of the pre-course briefing and/or projects and the post-course debriefing with their line manager?
5. To what extent do they feel that their line manager has been interested in their learning and their aims for its implementation?
6. Would they recommend the event/programme to their colleagues? In what terms and why? If not, why not?

Figure 13.8 *Key assessment questions about administration issues*

REPORTING THE EVALUATION RESULTS

Whether the evaluation process has been required by a client or stakeholder, eg a senior manager or the board, or is conducted by the training department as an essential part of their function, or if some form of training assessment has been made, it is advisable to record the results in a permanent form that can be referred to in the future. The training assessor or training manager may be required to present a report to the sponsors, stakeholders or senior management group.

There are many ways of producing reports, the format often being dictated by the culture of the organization, but three basic principles will always be useful:

- KISS – keep it short and simple
- Wherever possible use pictures, images, graphics rather than a lot of words or figures
- Identify the major stakeholders, your clients, and discover what their requirements or agenda might be

Emphasis has been placed on the necessity to report the results of analyses in textual, tabular or graphic chart form. If evaluation is performed, a permanent record should be kept, at the very least so that successive courses, events or programmes might be compared. But if the trainers' senior managers, training managers and the learners' line managers are interested in the results of the training they will wish to be kept informed of the progress of the evaluation. This will require a report in some form, usually with the tables and charts as described.

The simpler and more graphic the report, the more likely that it will be accepted.

KISS

It is only too easy, when you have generated a lot of statistical and quasi-statistical information and spent a lot of time on the evaluation of a training programme, to put everything into a report, even though this might result in a document many pages long. Resist the temptation and keep the report to the minimum possible, and there is a greater likelihood that it will be read and accepted. Winston Churchill is reported as demanding from his civil servants during World War II reports contained on one side of A4 paper. With a complex evaluation report this might be difficult, but brevity is possible by supporting the text (the main body of the report) with tables and charts as appendices. This gives the reader the opportunity of reading a brief but comprehensive report and referring to the supporting evidence only if they need/want to do so.

There are many publications and packages concerned with the skills involved in writing reports and you can refer to these if report writing is not one of your major skills. If the client is a demanding one in this respect, the report must be constructed in a form appropriate to the client, otherwise you run the risk of the report being rejected on style alone.

USING GRAPHICS

The type of material to be included in the report will usually dictate the form of any graphics or other images used. Evaluation reports will normally include tables and graphic representations of these, with organizational culture dictating which form of the graph is used – a line graph, block diagram, or whatever. It is tempting to introduce almost every type of graph into a single report – variety can increase interest, but overuse might suggest a flippant or 'clever' approach with consequent rejection.

Tabulated data

Table 13.1 is used to demonstrate the movement from difficult to read columns of figures to more acceptable graphics and is concerned with the number of unit trusts arranged during an eleven-year period.

Table 13.1 *Unit trust purchases*

	ORDINARY	SPECIAL	COMPLEX	TOTAL
	Millions of currency units			
1970	104,883	29,169	12,888	146,940
1971	110,322	34,088	14,000	158,410
1972	113,992	31,066	14,092	159,150
1973	128,534	36,304	14,308	179,146
1974	148,024	47,468	14,624	210,116
1975	186,970	47,170	14,592	248,732
1976	187,386	52,438	14,156	253,980
1977	189,388	61,636	14,102	265,126
1978	207,888	72,954	13,348	294,190
1979	227,000	78,658	12,908	318,566
1980	245,960	94,006	13,210	353,176
Totals	1,850,347	584,957	152,228	2,587,532

If you used this data within a report in the form of the table itself, very little benefit would result. The problems are that:

- there is too much detail included in one image to enable easy interpretation;
- breaking the table into several smaller tables would make description and comparison too difficult;
- the image is one of many large figures which dissolve into each other and make the eyes glaze over;
- if the readers are not fully conversant with the data (as is quite possible with your stakeholder senior manager) they cannot be expected to analyse the figures from this mass of information.

You are then faced with two problems to solve:

1. Which aspects of analysis do I want/need to demonstrate?
2. Which method of presentation is going to be the most effective for this kind of data?

Among other factors, the table demonstrates change. The horizontal totals show the change of the monetary value of purchases of unit trusts over a period of 11 years; the vertical totals show the relative size of purchases between ordinary, special and complex unit trusts. Both these aspects can be compared in a graphic.

In addition, the relative sizes of purchases of the three types of trust can be compared in each year; each figure can be converted to a percentage of its own column, its own year, or full totals of the decade or the type of trust. Any or all of these can be converted from the table to a graphic.

CHART FORMS

Any information can be presented in the form of a 'chart', a description commonly used for a range of charts, diagrams and drawings, each one being most effective when used for a particular purpose. The charts in most common use, and described here, include pie, bar, column and line charts and graphs.

Pie charts

A pie chart is a circle divided into segments, each segment showing a relative-sized part of the whole. Because all the information is included in the one circle, the pie chart is ideally suited to show at a glance a comparison of the components. However, with Table 13.1 in mind, the value of the pie would be destroyed if too many components were included; the pie works best with a simple approach, and an optimum of six or so components.

Positioning the components can be important. The eye is used to moving in a clockwise direction and to do so starts at about the 12 or 1 o'clock positions. Therefore it may be appropriate to place the segment which contains the most important information at this position, although this is not essential if the segments are clearly indicated.

The segments will be graded in size according to the size of the component being compared. This is best produced accurately, although approximate sizes can be used, provided these still demonstrate the relative differences in size.

Colours or shadings should be used to differentiate between each segment, although this is not completely essential as a line divides each segment. However, shading of some kind makes the segmentation more obvious, an essential element in a visual aid.

Figure 13.9 gives an example of two pie charts with information extracted from the Table 13.1. In the first (Figure 13.9a) the comparison is a simple one of the three components showing the total purchases of each type of unit in 1970. Ordinary units are 104,883 currency units = 71 per cent; special units are 29,169 = 20 per cent; complex units are 12,888 = 9 per cent.

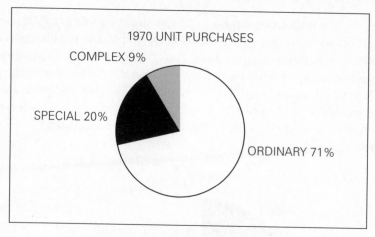

Figure 13.9(a) *A standard pie chart*

Figure 13.9(b) violates the suggestion that the optimum division of a pie is six or so components. However, in this case, the inclusion of 11 year segments is not too excessive to make the chart unreadable.

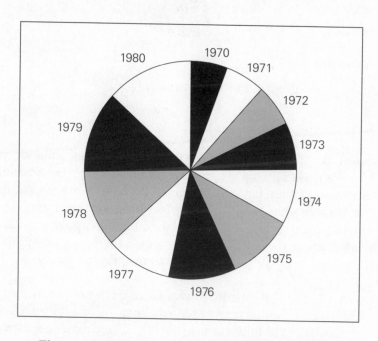

Figure 13.9(b) *A standard, multi-division pie chart*

There are a number of variations on the standard pie chart, the most useful and most frequently used being the exploded pie chart. In this version, the segment representing the component that the presenter wishes to make prominent is separated from the remainder of the pie. The separated segment can be at any place in the pie, and prominence is helped if the segment is positively shaded. Figure 13.10 is a representation of an exploded pie chart, again using the figures from Table 13.1.

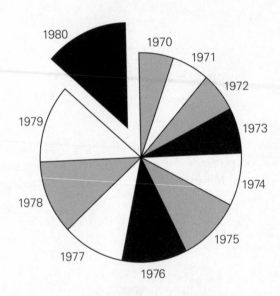

Figure 13.10   *An exploded pie chart*

Pie charts, because of their simplicity, can present information with impact. This makes them very suitable for images. Another advantage is that rarely do they have to be drawn by hand – every computer, however simple – has a software graphics program which enables pie charts to be constructed easily. Similar comments apply to virtually all the methods of presenting charts, so you have no argument for not using these by suggesting that there was insufficient time to produce them.

However, because of their simplicity, pie charts cannot show the finer details. Of course, captions can be placed alongside or within a segment giving information, but this starts to complicate the representation and make it unclear.

Bar charts

A bar chart can describe changes and comparisons in rather more detail than the pie chart. In its standard form it consists of a graph, but instead of depicting points on the graph (as in a line graph), each component is described with a block or bar. The chart can have two detailed dimensions or only one. In Figure 13.11 the total purchases are plotted against the years. Both the year and the amount of money involved are shown. In its simpler form, the money vertical dimension would be omitted, the height of the bar showing the relative differences between the years.

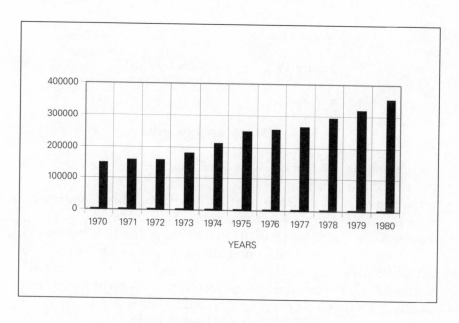

Figure 13.11   *A simple bar chart*

The bar chart in Figure 13.11 is presented with the bars vertical. This is the most frequently used method of drawing a bar chart, but many people consider it more effective if it is drawn so that the bars project horizontally from the left side vertical. The space below each bar in the vertical approach is strictly limited, particularly if there are an appreciable number of bars. In the horizontal version, much more text can be added, written within the bars, or, in the spaces between each bar. With simple information, such as the year in our example, additional space is not necessary so the vertical bar is satisfactory.

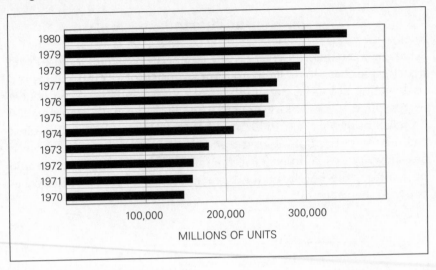

Figure 13.12 *A horizontal bar chart*

Line charts and graphs

The immediate reaction on the part of most people when a chart is suggested as a means of describing numerical data is to think of a graph. Line charts or graphs consist of information plotted on the vertical and horizontal axes with a point placed at the intersection of these axes. A continuous straight or curved line then joins the points.

Some simple rules ensure that the chart is as clear as possible. Usually the vertical scale represents magnitude or level and the horizontal scale time. The stages should be consistent in size and continuity – if data is missing a space should be left rather than ignoring its absence, otherwise the trends will be distorted.

There is no need to start the vertical scale always at zero; this can throw all the information into the top part of the graph, thus losing impact. Instead start with a scale point one step lower than the first point or with the first point at the intersection of the vertical and horizontal axes.

Graph constructors must always be aware of possible distortions introduced by using scales which are inconsistent with the information range – variable scale steps, omitted steps and exaggerated scales all manipulate the appearance of the graph and contaminate the visual impression. (These distortions are frequently used to attempt to give false impressions and can often be successful – political presentations are frequently perpetrators of this deception.)

Figure 13.13 is a typical line graph with the points joined by straight lines – the easiest although not always the best way of joining the points. In this case, the yearly totals of all units purchased are plotted against their monetary values.

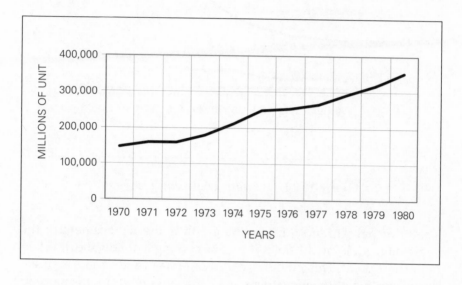

Figure 13.13   *A simple line graph*

Sometimes the reporter wants to produce a line graph showing the changing factors of a number of components, for example the growth of each of the unit trust types – ordinary, special and complex. Frequently this causes problems in the vertical size of the graph when, as in the case of the units, there is a large variation in the levels – the low-level complex figures will be close to the base of the graph and there will be a large gap between those and the figures for the ordinary units which will be at the top of the graph. On occasions this can be avoided by having two vertical scales for two components, one at the left, the other at the right. This works with two components, but with more than this there are unacceptable complications for an image constructor.

Unless a line graph is demanded, in these multiple cases it may be more appropriate to use another chart medium, for example a bar or column chart. However, in spite of the non-aesthetic nature of the multiple line graph with wide differences, these very differences may show the significance of the comparison between the components Figure 13.14 demonstrates this.

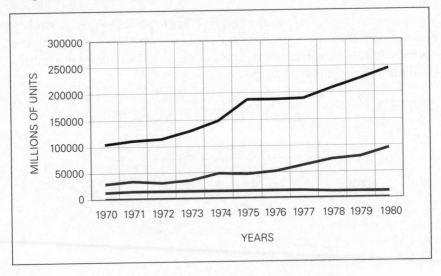

Figure 13.14 *A multi-component line graph*

The principal variation in the line graph is the replacement of the straight lines joining the points by a line curving to follow the direction of the next point. This produces a pleasant image and a more accurate demonstration of the movement, but requires good draughtsmanship to ensure these aspects.

There are of course numerous other types of charts, many for specific purposes, and if the charts discussed here do not satisfy your particular needs, you will need to refer to one of the specialist books on the subject. But remember that the more complex the chart the more difficult it is for the audience to understand it easily, and the more explanation you will have to give. Again bear in mind KISS!

THE MAJOR STAKEHOLDERS

The third major essential in producing an acceptable evaluation report (which, if necessary, will generate action for improvement by your stakeholders) is to ensure that the report you have produced is in the form that *they* want. If these stakeholders have an established interest in evaluation they will probably have strong views about it and they will want to see these areas covered. Providing information other than that required will not encourage them to 'own' the evaluation or the training. If they read the type of information they are expecting (not to be confused with your giving them everything they expect!), they will be more prepared to accept the report.

A FORMAT FOR THE REPORT

Evaluation reports may need to be formatted as required by the organizational culture, and their contents dictated by the extent of the validation and evaluation measures, and/or a training assessment. However, if this requirement does not exist – or you want to influence the organizational style if you feel it is not the most effective – there are standard approaches you can follow. One of these is summarized in Figure 13.15.

---

1. Contents.
2. A brief description of the subject of the report.
3. The reason for its production.
4. A summary of results.
5. A summary of recommendations.
6. A description of the methods used for data collection.
7. The main text.
8. Conclusions and recommendations.
9. Appendices.

Figure 13.15 *A summary of an example report format*

Contents

The inclusion of a contents section will be essential in almost every report, which may be several pages long. The section headings should be shown, followed by the page numbers and, if the Section is complex or lengthy and divided into sub-sections, a list of the headings of these sub-sections. The Content pages of this book demonstrate this approach, the sub-section headings acting almost as an index.

A brief description of the subject of the report

This section should briefly and concisely say what the report is about, eg 'This report is concerned with the results and recommendations relating to "X" training and development event (programme or open learning package) as the result of an evaluation project (or a training assessment).'

The reason for its production

Again this should not be too lengthy a section and should state:

1. Who authorized or requested the report.
2. Why the report is being produced and presented (eg 'because the first such-and-such a training programme had taken place and it needed to be assessed before further programmes were authorized'.
3. The criteria for the report production (eg 'the relevant material to be collated by the training manager who was then required to produce the report and submit it to the senior management board by "x" date').
4. A statement of the general action that was envisaged following presentation of the report (eg the relevant training manager would, by 'y' date, have the report returned with the various endorsements of the board for any necessary action).

A summary of results and recommendations

These summaries act as advance notification to the people receiving the report of the determinations and recommendations contained. They should simply state the text without explanations – these are proffered later in the report. Care should be taken at this stage, as it is very easy to add reasons or explanations for, perhaps, radical recommendations. This should be resisted, as too much material presented here can act against the reader reading the full report.

A description of the methods used for data collection

The data and graphics that demonstrate the validation and evaluation methods used are more properly located as appendices at the end of the report, apart from any that are essential in explaining the text. This section should therefore be a summary of the methods and instruments used, with clear references to the relevant appendices.

The main text

This can be the most substantial section of the report, and will usefully include comments on significant findings that were summarized earlier and general comments relating to their implications. The section can usefully follow a pattern of:

- a summary of each finding;
- interpretation of these results;
- implications of the findings;
- detailed recommendations.

Two options are usually available for the format within this pattern:

1. State the findings, their interpretation and implications, following each finding with recommendations relating to that finding.
2. List the findings, interpretations and implications as in (1), but leave the list of recommendations to be placed at the end of the section.

My own preference is for (1) as it seems to be tidier, keeping all appropriate material in one place.

Conclusions, including a reprise of the recommendations

This section can start with a general statement of the conclusions resulting from the examination of the material and any assessments and then contain a final *summary* of the recommendations. This reprise of the recommendations will be particularly helpful if in the preceding section the individual recommendations followed the text leading to them.

Appendices

This is the place for the example instruments: completed validation and evaluation instrument summaries and any material that can be omitted from the main text body without upsetting the flow and meaning of that text.

14

Customizing your Validation and Evaluation

Figure 2.1 summarized the training process from the suspected existence of a problem through to long-term assessment of the implementation of learned skills, including evaluation. This process describes the ideal situation which most training managers and trainers recognize as being desirable but very difficult to introduce in practice. Figure 2.2 concentrates on the evaluation cycle and suggests the full range of a *realistic* process of validation and evaluation.

It is apparent that there will be considerable variation in the extent to which evaluation is performed, due to a number of factors ranging from lack of interest in the process to a lack of resource and time. From the items in Figure 2.2 the evaluators can select the aspects that they feel are most relevant to their situation and for which resources are available. Some of these decisions will be seen by some people as having less value than a full evaluation, even of having no value. But I believe that *any* evaluation approach is of *some* value, particularly if it is applied consistently so that comparisons can be made over time. Obviously the more detailed and in depth the evaluation, the more effective it should be, but you must be satisfied with what you are able to do. This does not exclude (using evaluation evidence as part of the argument) trying to persuade senior management for sufficient resources to enable a fuller approach to be attempted.

A number of specific approaches can be identified. This chapter describes those from the simplest (in which nothing is done), through an increasing complexity of methods, to a full evaluation process. All presume that the early stages of the full training process, namely identification of needs and design of the training programme, have been performed, and most require the education of line managers to give maximum support to the evaluation. The basic criterion is that evaluation is not for the trainer alone to carry out, but is the province of the training quintet.

APPROACH ONE

At the most elementary end of the consideration of evaluation is the situation where no validation or evaluation is attempted. This may be due to a lack of interest on the part of the training practitioners or their clients or stakeholders, or specifically the latter, as a result of which no resources are available. In the former case, the earlier chapters of this book should be read again. With clients and stakeholders, as suggested above, a case might be made (again perhaps using the earlier material in this book), for the authorization of resources. It may be, of course, that the senior levels of management are totally uninterested. The training practitioners then have alternatives:

- to accept the constraints and reflect the lack of interest in the non-evaluation;
- to accept the higher level attitudes, but try to do some evaluation in spite of this, if only for their own peace of mind.

APPROACH TWO

This is probably the simplest approach that will offer some element of evaluation with the minimum use of resources. The approach concentrates principally on the reactions of the learners to the learning event and, because feelings and opinions only are being sought, there is little real validation. However, some information useful and helpful to consideration of the future of the programme can be obtained by this method.

Although the instrument used is a reactionnaire it should be as far removed as possible from the 'happy' sheet and it should be given an important place in the programme. A suitable instrument for this approach is part three (either alternative, although the first is recommended) of Figure 9.1.

What should be a common aspect of *all* training programmes is the completion of and commitment to an action plan. Although not directly an evaluation instrument, the action plan can reflect the learners' attitudes to the programme and its content and value as a learning event. The request for the learners to complete an action plan will reinforce the value of the learning and help towards the commitment of the learners to implementing their learning.

Approach Two

1. Use a reactionnaire, such as Figure 9.1, part three, at the end of the training programme
2. Have the learners complete action plans at the end of the training programme

APPROACH THREE

This is the next stage up and introduces a reasonably realistic attempt to include validation and evaluation. There is little extra resource involvement than that needed in Approach Two, since the only difference is that the full instrument shown in Figure 9.1 is used. This extension, however, starts to concentrate on *learning* rather simply than reaction to the training. If the learning stated is minimal or varies significantly from the objectives of the training programme, there is something wrong with the programme. It may be that the content is wrong, the level is pitched too high, the level is pitched too low, the wrong people are attending; and so on, and some form of more in-depth investigation is called for.

Time *must* be built into the training programme to allow this document to be completed effectively, rather than the all too frequent, last-minute handing out of a questionnaire, almost as the learners are leaving the training. The value and importance of the approach should be stressed by the trainer so that there is a maximum chance that the questionnaires will be completed fully and honestly. The responses also give good indications of the effectiveness of the training programme: if the scoring and comments relate to the lower end of the range this indicates, as suggested earlier, that there is something wrong with either the construction of the programme or the learning population. If the good learning comments suggest aspects that were not intended from the objectives of the programme, again there are validation indications – it may be that emphasis was placed during the programme on subjects other than those intended in its initial design, rightly or wrongly. The trainer will need to investigate these indications, whatever they may be.

Approach Three

1. Use a questionnaire such as the complete Figure 9.1 at the end of the programme
2. Have the learners complete action plans at the end of the training programme

---

APPROACH FOUR

The line manager is brought into the evaluation process in this approach, an essential move for a full and effective evaluation, although the problems and difficulties must not be ignored or minimized. In many organizations it may be that an educative process needs to be introduced to encourage line managers to accept their responsibilities and commit themselves to supporting fully both the training of their staff and the evaluation process. Without the commitment of line managers to even the minimal involvement suggested in this approach there is little hope for anything more extensive. The approach takes Approach Three one stage further with pre-programme and post-programme meetings between the line managers and the learners.

Approach Four

1. Pre-programme briefing meeting of line manager and learner. Figure 3.3 gives guidelines for the format and content of this meeting
2. Use Figure 9.1 in its complete form at the end of the programme
3. Have the learners complete action plans at the end of the training programme
4. Post-programme debriefing meeting of line manager and learner. Figure 3.4 gives guidelines for the format and content of this meeting

---

APPROACH FIVE

Approaches Two to Four have concentrated on obtaining some form of learner feedback by the use of end of programme questionnaires, reactionnaires and action plans, plus the involvement before and after the programme of the line manager. These approaches will be useful when:

- it is not necessary to assess pre-training skill, knowledge and attitude levels because the content of the programme is completely new and it may safely be assumed that the learners are all starting from a zero point;
- there is no opportunity, for whatever reason, to assess a starting level.

However, wherever possible it is essential that some form of starting position should be assessed, otherwise the end of programme 'measures' mean nothing other than to give some indication of the quality of the training, rather than the learning. As described earlier, this pre- or start of programme assessment can be achieved by tests, demonstrations, practical activities, self-assessments and so on, a record being kept of the results so that end of programme comparisons can be made and the extent of learning assessed. Reference for the most appropriate instruments should be made to Chapters 4, 5 and 6.

Approach Five

1. **Pre-programme briefing meeting of line manager and learner. Figure 3.3 gives guidelines for the format and content of this meeting**
2. **Pre-programme or start of programme testing or other assessment to identify learners' starting levels. These resources are described in Chapters 4, 5 and 6**
3. **Use Figure 9.1 in its complete form at the end of the programme**
    Have the learners complete action plans at the end of the training programme
4. **Post-programme debriefing meeting of line manager and learner. Figure 3.4 gives guidelines for the format and content of this meeting**

APPROACH SIX

This approach is particularly relevant in the case of programmes that have durations of longer than one or two days. It suggests the use of one or more of the interim assessments described in Chapter 7, either in the form of spot checks, diurnal audits or Learning Logs. Remember the caveat of including an interim assessment only when action can be taken as a result of the review when this is called for.

Approach Six

1. Pre-programme briefing meeting of line manager and learner. Figure 3.3 gives guidelines for the format and content of this meeting
2. Pre-programme or start of programme testing or other assessment to identify learners' starting levels. These resources are described in Chapters 4, 5 and 6
3. Use an interim validation, evaluation or assessment resource where this is relevant, such as those described in Chapter 7
4. Use Figure 9.1 in its complete form at the end of the programme
5. Have the learners complete action plans at the end of the training programme
6. Post-programme debriefing meeting of line manager and learner. Figure 3.4 gives guidelines for the format and content of this meeting

---

APPROACH SEVEN

This is a simple modification to Approach Six, which can be useful in training programmes that concentrate on interactive skills or people skills and which are not suitable for objective forms of assessment. Approach Five introduces the start of programme audits; one of these is the self-assessment pre-post-test which in the majority of cases is improved in value by extending it to the three-test format. Obviously, the use of the three-test requires more programme time, not only for its completion, but also for discussion of the results. However, in 'people' types of programmes, such a test is essential.

Approach Seven

1. Pre-programme briefing meeting of line manager and learner. Figure 3.3 gives guidelines for the format and content of this meeting
2. Pre-programme or start of programme testing or other assessment to identify learners' starting levels. These resources are described in Chapters 4, 5 and 6
3. If relevant to the type of training, use the three-test self-assessment instrument at the end of the programme as described in Chapter 8 and Figure 6.7
4. Use an interim validation, evaluation or assessment resource where this is relevant, such as those in Chapter 7
5. If relevant to the type of training, use the three-test self-assessment instrument at the end of the programme as described in Chapter 8 and Figure 6.7
6. Use Figure 9.1 in its complete form at the end of the programme
7. Have the learners complete action plans at the end of the training programme
8. Post-programme debriefing meeting of line manager and learner. Figure 3.4 gives guidelines for the format and content of this meeting

APPROACH EIGHT

This approach is the summation of the various approaches described above, completed by medium- and longer-term evaluations. It is obvious that substantial resources are required to perform this approach, but equally obvious that, if evaluation is performed in this manner, every form of evidence required to answer the questions 'Does your training do what it is supposed to do?' and 'Is it worth it?' will be available.

Approach Eight

1. Pre-programme briefing meeting of line manager and learner. Figure 3.3 gives guidelines for the format and content of this meeting
2. Pre-programme or start of programme testing or other assessment to identify learners' starting levels. These resources are described in Chapters 4, 5 and 6
3. If relevant to the type of training, use the three-test self-assessment instrument at the end of the programme as described in Chapter 8 and Figure 6.7
4. Use an interim validation, evaluation or assessment resource where this is relevant, such as those in Chapter 7
5. If relevant to the type of training, use the three-test self-assessment instrument at the end of the programme as described in Chapter 8 and Figure 6.7
6. Use Figure 9.1 in its complete form at the end of the programme
7. Have the learners complete action plans at the end of the training programme
8. Post-programme debriefing meeting of line manager and learner. Figure 3.4 gives guidelines for the format and content of this meeting
9. Perform medium- and longer-term evaluation concentrating on the implementation of learning as suggested by the learners' action plans, as described in Chapter 11 and Figures 11.1 to 11.4 and 11.6
   (a) Send letter of enquiry to learners seeking information about implementation of the action plans
   (b) Send letter of enquiry to learners and their line managers seeking information about implementation of the action plans
   (c) Conduct telephone interviews with learners about implementation of the action plans
   (d) Conduct telephone interviews with learners and their line managers about implementation of the action plans
   (e) Conduct face-to-face interviews with learners about implementation of the action plans
   (f) Conduct face-to-face interviews with learners and their line managers about implementation of the action plans

CONCLUSION

This final chapter has suggested a range of ways in which the guidelines described in the earlier part of the book can be applied to validation and evaluation of a variety of training and learning programmes. Within the eight approaches described, most practitioners will find a process that suits their particular situation, or a process of mix-and-match can be employed. Evaluation need not be too complicated or over-expensive in resource terms, and can be valuable if you use it within the constraints of your resources and organizational demands. At the very least it tells you as a practitioner that you are achieving what you set out to achieve and your learners are benefiting from your training offering; but it can also provide evidence to prove these achievements to your clients, stakeholders or senior managers who might require you to do so. Resources for training and development are always under threat, but if their high value can be shown rather than described by optimistic statements, they should be that much safer.

References and Recommended Reading

Bartram, Sharon and Gibson, Brenda (1994) *Training Needs Analysis*, Gower.

Bee, Frances and Bee, Roland (1994) *Training Needs Analysis and Evaluation*, Institute of Personnel and Development.

Bramley, Peter (1990) *Evaluating Training Effectiveness*, McGraw-Hill.

Craig, Malcolm (1994) *Analysing Learning Needs*, Gower.

Easterby-Smith, Mark (1980) 'How to use repertory grids in HRD', *Journal of European Industrial Training*, Vol 4, No 2.

Easterby-Smith, Mark (1994) *Evaluating Management Development, Education and Training* (2nd edn), Gower.

Fletcher, Shirley (1994) *NVQs Standards and Competence*, (2nd edn), Kogan Page.

Hamblin, A C (1974) *The Evaluation and Control of Training*, McGraw-Hill.

Honey, Peter (1979) 'The repertory grid in action', *Industrial and Commercial Training*, Vol II, Nos 9–11.

Honey, Peter (1988) *Face to Face*, Gower.

Honey, Peter (1994) *Learning Log: A way to enhance learning from experience*, Honey Publications.

Kelly, G A (1953) *The Psychology of Personal Constructs*, Norton.

Kirkpatrick, Donald L (1996) 'Evaluation of Training' in R L Craig (ed) *Training and Development Handbook*, McGraw-Hill.

Newby, Tony (1992a) *Training Evaluation Handbook*, Gower.

Newby, Tony (1992b) *Validating Your Training*, Kogan Page Practical Trainer Series.

Peterson, Robyn (1992) *Training Needs Analysis in the Workplace*, Kogan Page Practical Trainer Series.

Prior, John (ed) (1994) *Handbook of Training and Development*, (2nd edn), Gower.

Rackham, N and Morgan, T (1977) *Behaviour Analysis in Training*, McGraw-Hill.

Rackham, N and others (1971) *Developing Interactive Skills*, Wellens.

Rae, L (1983) 'Towards a more valid end-of-course validation', *Training Officer*, October.

Rae, L (1984) 'The validation of training', *Training and Development*, May.

Rae, L (1985) *The Skills of Human Relations Training*, Gower.

Rae, L (1991) *Assessing Trainer Effectiveness*, Gower.

Rae, L (1995) *Techniques of Training*, (3rd edn), Gower, (Chapter 10).

Rae, L (1997) *How to Measure Training Effectiveness*, (3rd edn), Gower.

Reay, David G (1995) *Evaluating Training*, Kogan Page.

Scriven, M (1974) 'Evaluation perspectives and procedures' in W J Popham, *Evaluation in Education*, McCuthlan Corporation.

Wade, Pamela (1995) *Measuring the Impact of Training*, Chang/Kogan Page.

Warr, P B, Bird, M and Rackham, N (1970) *The Evaluation of Management Training*, Gower.

Whitelaw, M (1972) *The Evaluation of Management Training: A review*, IPM.

Wills, Mike (1993) *Managing the Training Process*, McGraw-Hill.

Index

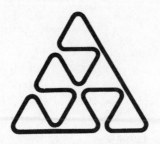